The Cost of Doing Business Study

2008 Edition

Prepared by
NAHB Economics Group

Sponsored by

biztools
Business Management & Information
Technology Committee

Grant Thornton
A passion for the business of accounting®

BuilderBooks.com®
BOOKS THAT BUILD YOUR BUSINESS

A Service of
NAHB
NATIONAL ASSOCIATION
OF HOME BUILDERS

The Cost of Doing Business Study 2008 Edition

BuilderBooks, a Service of the National Association of Home Builders

Courtenay S. Brown	Director, Book Publishing
Doris M. Tennyson	Senior Editor
Natalie C. Holmes	Book Editor
Torrie Singletary	Production Editor
Open Soul Design	Cover Design
Circle Graphics	Composition
Hamilton Printing	Printing
Gerald M. Howard	NAHB Executive Vice President and CEO
Mark Pursell	NAHB Senior Staff Vice President, Marketing & Sales Group
Lakisha Campbell	NAHB Staff Vice President, Publications & Affinity Programs

NAHB Economics Group

Gopal Ahluwalia	Staff Vice President, Research
Rose Quint	Assistant Staff Vice President, Research

NAHB Business Management Department

Agustín Cruz	Executive Director
Joshua Nester	Communications Manager
Marcia Childs	Education and Resource Manager
Germaine Palangdao	Home Technology Alliance Program Manager
Trevor Lynch	Business Management Intern

Printed in the United States of America

12 11 10 09 08   1 2 3 4 5

ISBN-13: 978-0-86718-636-9

Library of Congress CIP information available on request.

For further information, please contact:

BuilderBooks.com
BOOKS THAT BUILD YOUR BUSINESS

A Service of NAHB
National Association of Home Builders

National Association of Home Builders
1201 15th Street, NW
Washington, DC 20005-2800
800-223-2665
www.BuilderBooks.com.

Contents

Figures

Tables

Chapter 5. Small-Volume Builders

Chapter 6. Production Builders

Chapter 9. Historical Perspective

Chapter 11. The Balance Sheet: A Tool for Measuring, Managing Risk

Chapter 13. Financial Ratios: Valuable Management Tools for All Home Builders

Acknowledgments

NAHB thanks the builders who provided their companies' valuable financial information for the 15th edition of the *Cost of Doing Business Study*. This study would not have been possible without their time and effort. In addition, NAHB's Business Management & Information Technology Committee would like to thank Grant Thornton for generously sponsoring the *Cost of Doing Business Study 2008 Edition*.

The following members of the Financial Management Issues Work Group of the Business Management & Information Technology Committee shared their insights and suggested many improvements to the 2008 edition of the study:

Bill Murray, Chair, The Robert Criswell Co.
Bill Allen, William Drew Consulting
David Asbridge, Highmark Publishers
Chuck Austin, Austin Signature Homes
John Barrows, J. Barrows Inc.
Maggie Geoffrey, Construction Data Control Inc.
Alan Hanbury, Jr., CGR, CAPS, House of Hanbury Builders Inc.
Alex Hannigan, Hannigan Homes Inc.
Steven Hays, Sr., CPA, Rubin Brown LLP
Mark Hutchings, PhD, Brigham Young University
Dallas Johnson, Dalmac Homes Inc.
Joel B. Katz, GMB, CPA, Katz Builders Inc.
Lucy T. Katz, CAPS, Katz Builders Inc.
Mike J. Kegley, Bold Homes Inc.
Steve Maltzman, CPA, SMA Consulting
Richard Miles, Dogwood Homes

Leslie Mostow, Reznick Group
Randy Noel, Reve, Inc.
Jim Patrick, Dolphin Construction
Ron Robichaud, Robichaud Associates
Jim Sattler, Jim Sattler Construction
Don Scattergood, Mark Systems
Manny Schatz, PBS Inc.
Paul Scholes, Moser Builders Inc.
Tim Shigley, Shigley Construction Co.
Emma Shinn, MBA, CPA, Shinn Consulting
Chris Thompson, On The Level Inc.
Steven Washburn, Washburn Custom Builders
Rusty Wysocki, Rusty Wysocki Building Co.

We also thank the following contributing writers and reviewers:

Alan Hanbury, Jr., CGR, CAPS, House of Hanbury Builders Inc.
Steven Hays, Sr., CPA, Rubin Brown LLP
Mary Alice Hewitt, NAHB
Ron Robichaud, Robichaud Associates
Emma Shinn, MBA, CPA, Shinn Consulting

Introduction

Is the risk associated with your home building business investment worth the profit reward that you are getting? Could you, or should you, be earning more from your business? Are you an "average Joe" or a builder who will stand above the crowd when the time comes to sell your business? Where should you be cutting costs or investing more? The *Cost of Doing Business Study,* conducted 15 times since 1970, can help you answer these questions. Builders like you have provided the financial data for this study, including their *gross profit, net profit,* expenses, and revenue. The study is a window into the operating costs and profitability of small, medium, and large single-family and attached home building businesses.

The study is based on the results of a survey conducted by the National Association of Home Builders (NAHB) in 2007. Nearly 300 NAHB builder members graciously participated by providing their companies' 2006 financial data. The NAHB Business Management & Information Technology Committee guided the survey's creation and reviewed and commented on the draft manuscript. The NAHB Economics Group conducted the survey and tabulated the findings, while the NAHB Business Management Department compiled the final manuscript. Grant Thornton sponsored the study.

Various categories of builders as well as financial terms used throughout the study, italicized on first text reference, are defined in the glossary on pages 73–74.

A Benchmark for Building Businesses

The *Cost of Doing Business Study* offers builders important insights about their businesses, allowing them to see how they rank among peers in the industry and to gain historical perspective on industry performance.

Benchmarking, comparing one company's business systems and results with others', can suggest areas for improvement, help to set budget targets, and provide a roadmap for boosting profitability and increasing efficiency. More than a statistical report, the *Cost of Doing Business Study* provides one benchmark to compare an individual company's financial performance with that of similar businesses and with the industry as a whole.

The study examines key statistics that are critical to business success—gross and net profit—and isolates these and other findings for various categories of builders, so that readers can make valid comparisons. Some builder categories may overlap and builders' financial data may appear in more than one category. For example, the study examines performance by volume and by whether builders had land costs.[1] It also looks at the top and bottom 25% of builders by their net profits.

Expenditures are analyzed by the following categories:

- land
- direct construction
- indirect construction
- financing
- sales and marketing
- general and administrative
- owner's compensation

To make the most of this study, gather your financial information, beginning with your latest *income statement* and *balance sheet;* then, look at how your company's performance compares with that of similar builders. Is your net profit higher, lower, or about average compared with other home building businesses? Is your gross profit higher or lower than the industry averages? Were your line-item expenses distributed in the same way as those of other builders?

---

[1] Note: Breakdowns for small-volume and production builders without land costs could not be reported because of a low response rate.

By comparing your results with those of others in the industry, you can identify strengths and weaknesses in your company. Comparing your company's numbers with those of your peers reveals where yours might lag, thus pointing the way for future improvement. Following are suggestions for using the information you learn about your company's performance from the *Cost of Doing Business Study:*

- Consider industry numbers in setting budgets and targets.
- Use the study as a basis for spending in broad categories, or specific departments, within your company.
- Reference the findings in discussions with potential lenders. If your company is better than—or even at—industry averages in particular areas, present these findings to negotiate better loan terms or interest rates.
- Use the study to provide an objective measurement for establishing a company reward system.

Industry Profitability

On average, the study reveals that 2006 was on par with 2005, even though the industry began to experience decreases in traffic and in new sales contracts, and more cancellations, during the second half of 2006. Fortunately, the momentum of 2005 carried over somewhat into 2006 and allowed most builders to maintain their levels of performance. However, NAHB's Economics Group is anticipating a considerable short-term decline in profitability going forward. This altered environment requires builders to adjust their organizations and pay attention to cash flow as well as gross margins.

How profitable were builders who answered the 2007 *Cost of Doing Business* survey?

- Average gross profit was 20.9%
- Average net profit was 7.7%

These profits are consistent with survey findings from previous years, which are summarized in Chapter 9.

Builders ask, "What kinds of profits should my company be earning?" There really is no hard-and-fast rule for every building business. Even the averages presented in the *Cost of Doing Business Study* are not necessarily appropriate goals for every company. Keeping these caveats in mind, industry experts encourage home builders to aim for gross margins of 22%–27% and net profits of 8%–15%. However, many companies post higher numbers, whereas many do not achieve these levels. Therefore, do not make abrupt changes in your business based on industry ideals and the information in this book. In particular, consider the costs of increasing volume as well as the potential increase in gross profit, as Alan Hanbury recommends in Chapter 12. Likewise, do not assume that your market will accept large price increases. The key is to build on current successes, not to change for the sake of change.

The most important tool available for analyzing building business operations is an annual operating budget that an owner reviews monthly against actual performance. Conducting these ongoing reviews helps builders stay in control of their company's financials, reduces surprises, and maximizes profitability. Of course, financial information is not the only measure of a building company's performance. Construction quality, management performance, and timeliness of pre- and post-construction systems also matter. All of these can be measured and improved.

To comment on the *Cost of Doing Business Study: 2008 Edition* or suggest improvements for the next edition, contact:

NAHB Business Management Department
1201 15th Street, NW
Washington, D.C. 20005
(800) 368-5242 x8388
business_management@nahb.com

1

All Survey Respondents

The *Cost of Doing Business Study* survey questionnaire was mailed to 3,367 builders in March 2007. The questionnaire requested 2006 financial and operational information as well as details about the type of single-family units closed in 2006. With the exception of one survey question that asked builders to quantify their "main" and "other" operations, the *Cost of Doing Business Study* is based only on responses from single-family home builders who said single-family production or custom home building were their main or secondary operations.

NAHB received 290 responses, a response rate of 8.6%. Every question was not answered by all respondents. Table 1.1 breaks down the responses by U.S. Census region, type of builder, and number of single-family homes closed in 2006.[2]

Regionally, the largest proportion of respondents (41%) was in the South. The next largest group, 28%, was in the Midwest. Seventeen percent of respondents were in the West and 14% were in the Northeast.

The largest proportion of respondents (46%) had land as well as construction costs: they built for sale on land they developed or purchased. *Combination builders,* who built both on their own land and on property their customers owned, accounted for 35% of the survey responses. Finally, 19% of respondents built exclusively on land their customers owned, so they had no land costs in their construction businesses.

By volume, most respondents were *small-volume builders*. Sixty-five percent closed 25 or fewer homes in 2006, and 44% of small-volume

---

[2] Due to rounding, the numbers in the tables presented throughout the study may not total 100%.

1

Table 1.1 Respondents' profile

	% of total
Region	
Northeast: Connecticut, Maine, Massachusetts, New Hampshire, New Jersey, New York, Pennsylvania, Rhode Island, Vermont	14
Midwest: Illinois, Indiana, Iowa, Kansas, Michigan, Minnesota, Missouri, Nebraska, North Dakota, Ohio, South Dakota, Wisconsin	28
South: Alabama, Arkansas, Delaware, District of Columbia, Florida, Georgia, Kentucky, Louisiana, Maryland, Mississippi, North Carolina, Oklahoma, South Carolina, Tennessee, Texas, Virginia, West Virginia	41
West: Alaska, Arizona, California, Colorado, Hawaii, Idaho, Montana, Nevada, New Mexico, Oregon, Utah, Washington, Wyoming	17
Type of builder	
With land costs	46
Without land costs	19
Combination	35
Single-family homes closed in 2006	
<10	44
10–25	21
26–99	24
≥100	11

builders closed fewer than 10. (The remaining 21% of small-volume builders closed 10–25 homes.) The largest proportion of survey respondents (24%) closed 26–99 homes, and builders who closed 100 or more single-family homes were the smallest proportion of the survey pool (11%). In terms of revenue, the largest proportion of respondents (37%) earned $10 million or more in 2006. The next largest group (28%) earned less than $2 million. Twenty-three percent earned $2–$4.9 million, and 12% earned $5–$9.9 million.

Income Statement and Balance Sheet

The *Cost of Doing Business Study* survey asked respondents for data from their 2006 income statement, including revenues and expenses. On the revenue side, the survey asked for income from single-family or multi-family building. On the expense side, the survey asked for the *cost of goods sold*, which includes land and *operating expenses* (Appendix II).

To examine *owner's equity*, the survey asked respondents about assets and liabilities as well; specifically, how much money the company had in cash, the amount tied to construction work in progress, and the amounts

Table 1.2 Gross profit

	Average (in $1,000s)	Share of revenue (%)
Revenue	18,686	100.0
Cost of goods sold		
Land costs	2,929	15.7
Direct costs: single family	9,809	52.5
Direct costs: multifamily, remodeling, light commercial/industrial	1,054	5.6
Indirect construction costs	605	3.2
Other costs	402	2.2
Total cost of goods sold	14,799	79.2
Gross profit	**3,887**	**20.8**

owed in current liabilities or in construction loans (Appendix I). This data is summarized in balance sheet tables.

Total revenue averaged $18.7 million. The cost of goods sold was $14.8 million, or 79.2% of revenue. Therefore, average gross profit was $3.9 million, a 20.8% *gross profit margin* (table 1.2).

Operating expenses averaged $2.5 million or 13.1% of revenue (table 1.3).

After operating expenses, the average net income among survey respondents was $1.4 million, a *net profit margin* of 7.7% (fig. 1.1).

Survey respondents' total assets averaged $12.9 million. Of that amount, respondents had an average of $9.6 million invested in construction work

Table 1.3 Net profit

	Average (in $1,000s)	Share of revenue (%)
Gross profit	3,887	20.8
Operating expenses		
Financing expenses	462	2.5
Sales & marketing expenses	827	4.4
General & administrative expenses	927	5.0
Owner's compensation	239	1.3
Total operating expenses	2,456	13.1
Net profit	**1,431**	**7.7**

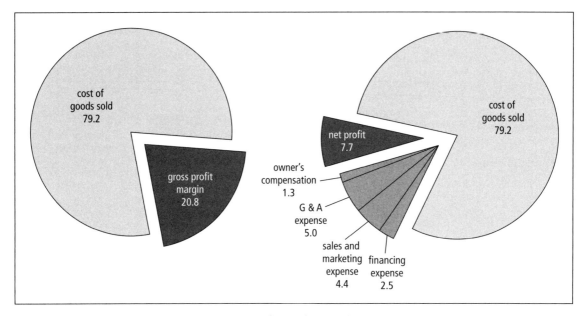

Figure 1.1 Cost of goods sold, expenses, and net profit (% of revenue)

in progress and $823,000 in cash. They held an additional $1.1 million in other current assets and $1.4 million in other assets. On the liabilities side, respondents owed on average $6.3 million in construction loans, and $1.8 million in other current liabilities. In all, liabilities averaged $9.5 million and owner's equity averaged $3.4 million (table 1.4).

Table 1.4 Balance sheet

	Average (in $1,000s)	Share of total (%)
Assets		
Current assets		
Cash	823	6.4
Construction work in progress	9,635	74.3
Other current assets	1,120	8.6
Total current assets	11,578	89.3
Other assets	1,382	10.7
Total assets	**12,959**	**100.0**
Median total assets	3,553	
Liabilities		
Current liabilities	1,792	13.8
Construction loans	6,318	48.8
Total current liabilities	8,110	62.6
Other liabilities	1,438	11.0
Total liabilities	**9,548**	**73.7**
Owner's equity	**3,411**	**26.3**
Median owner's equity	491	

Table 1.5 Financial ratios

Current ratio	1.43 to 1
Debt-to-equity ratio	2.8 to 1
Return on assets	11%
Return on equity	42%

Respondents averaged a *current ratio* of 1.43 to 1 and a *debt-to-equity ratio* of 2.8 to 1. Returns on assets and equity show how well a company is utilizing its invested capital. For all respondents, the return on assets was 11% and return on equity was 42% (table 1.5).

Top and Bottom 25%

To compare results between the most and the least successful builders (in terms of profitability), responses were tabulated independently for two distinct groups of firms: the top 25% and the bottom 25%, as measured by their net profit margins.

Builders in the top 25% had average revenue of $27.1 million, average gross profit of $7 million, and a 25.9% gross profit margin. Their operating expenses consumed 12.3% of earnings, leaving a net profit margin of 13.7%. Owner's compensation was 1.1% of revenue.

On the other hand, builders in the bottom 25% had average revenue of $10.8 million, gross profit of $1.3 million, and a gross profit margin of 12.2%. Their operating expenses were $1.4 million, or 13.2% of revenue. This group's net profit margin was 1% (fig. 1.2).

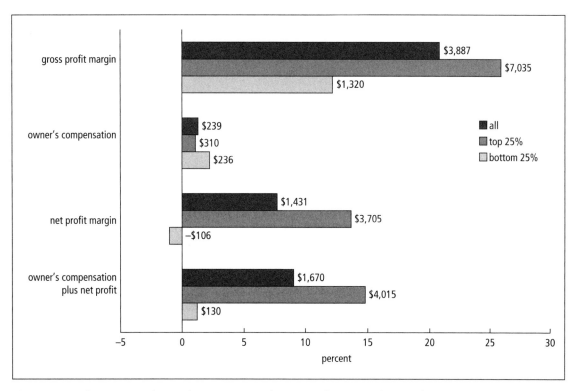

Figure 1.2 Profit margins and owner's compensation (average in $1,000s and as % of revenue)

Table 1.6 Top and bottom 25%

	Top 25%	All	Bottom 25%
Gross profit margin	25.9%	20.8%	12.2%
Net profit margin	13.7%	7.7%	−1.0%
Current ratio	1.50 to 1	1.43 to 1	1.17 to 1
Debt-to-equity ratio	2.05 to 1	2.80 to 1	3.99 to 1
Return on assets	20.5%	11.0%	−0.8%
Return on equity	62.7%	42.0%	−4.1%

The 2006 balance sheet for the top 25% of respondents shows they had an average of $18 million in total assets, $12.1 million in liabilities, and average equity of $5.9 million. Builders in the bottom 25%, on the other hand, had an average of $12.9 million in assets, $10.4 million in liabilities, and average equity of $2.6 million (Appendix I). Table 1.6 summarizes important statistics from the income statement and balance sheet for the top and bottom 25% of all respondents.

2

Builders With Land Costs

Survey respondents that built on land they developed or purchased averaged $27.6 million in revenues, $21.5 million in cost of goods sold, average gross profit of $6.1 million, and a 22.1% gross profit margin. Their cost of goods sold consumed 77.9% of revenue (table 2.1). Operating expenses averaged $3.6 million for *builders with land costs*, which consumed 13% of their revenue (table 2.2).

After subtracting operating expenses from gross profits, builders with land costs averaged a net profit of $2.5 million, 9.1% of total revenue. Figure 2.1 summarizes the income statement for builders with land costs.

Builders with land costs held an average of $19.3 million in total assets: $14.8 million in construction work in progress, $1.3 million in cash, and $1.4 million in other current assets such as refundable deposits and furnished model homes. On the liabilities side, they had an average of $9.4 million in construction loans and $1.8 million in additional current liabilities. The remaining $2.5 million was other liabilities such as long-term notes payable and deferred income tax. Total liabilities were $13.7 million (71% of assets) and equity averaged $5.6 million (29% of assets) (table 2.3).

Builders with land costs averaged a current ratio of 1.56 to 1 and a debt-to-equity ratio of 2.44 to 1. Return on assets was 12.9% and return on equity was 44.5% (table 2.4).

Top and Bottom 25% of Builders With Land Costs

Among builders with land costs, the most profitable group (top 25%) reported an average of $39.5 million in total revenue and an average gross

7

Table 2.1 Gross profit

	Average (in $1,000s)	Share of revenue (%)
Revenue	27,564	100.0
Cost of goods sold		
Land costs	4,671	16.9
Direct costs: single family	14,342	52.0
Direct costs: multifamily, remodeling, light		
commercial/industrial	837	3.1
Indirect construction costs	856	3.1
Other costs	774	2.8
Total cost of goods sold	21,481	77.9
Gross profit	**6,083**	**22.1**

profit of $10.9 million. This represents a 27.7% gross profit margin. Operating expenses consumed 12% of revenue, leaving a net profit margin of 15.6% (fig. 2.2).

In comparison, builders with land costs whose financial performance was in the bottom 25% reported average total revenue of $14.5 million and average cost of goods sold of $12.5 million. Their gross profit was $2 million and their gross margin was 13.8%. After accounting for operating expenses (13.8% of revenue), this group of builders had a net profit of $11,000 and a net profit margin of 0.1%.

Table 2.2 Net profit

	Average (in $1,000s)	Share of revenue (%)
Gross profit	6,083	22.1
Operating expenses		
Financing expenses	737	2.7
Sales & marketing expenses	1,241	4.5
General & administrative expenses	1,299	4.7
Owner's compensation	311	1.1
Total operating expenses	3,587	13.0
Net profit	**2,496**	**9.1**

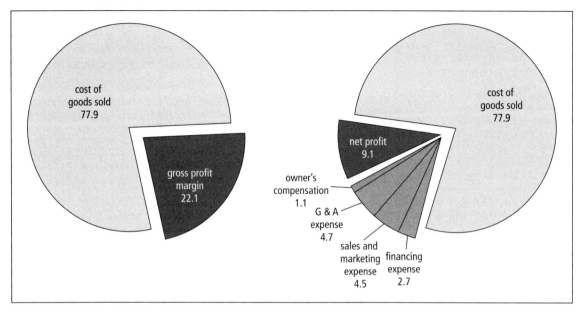

Figure 2.1 Cost of goods sold, expenses, and net profit (% of revenue)

Table 2.3 Balance sheet

	Average (in $1,000s)	Share of total (%)
Assets		
Current assets		
Cash	1,286	6.7
Construction work in progress	14,790	76.5
Other current assets	1,430	7.4
Total current assets	17,506	90.6
Other assets	1,822	9.4
Total assets	**19,327**	**100.0**
Median total assets	8,478	
Liabilities		
Current liabilities	1,773	9.2
Construction loans	9,417	48.7
Total current liabilities	11,190	57.9
Other liabilities	2,525	13.1
Total liabilities	**13,715**	**71**
Owner's equity	**5,613**	**29**
Median owner's equity	1,170	

Table 2.4 Financial ratios

Current ratio	1.56 to 1
Debt-to-equity ratio	2.44 to 1
Return on assets	12.9%
Return on equity	44.5%

The 2006 balance sheet for the top 25% of builders with land costs shows they had an average of $24.9 million in total assets. With total liabilities averaging $15.3 million, these builders had average equity of $9.6 million. Builders with land costs who were in the bottom 25% in terms of net profit margins reported average total assets of $20.1 million, liabilities of $15.3 million, and average equity of $4.8 million (Appendix I). Table 2.5 summarizes important statistics from the income statement and balance sheet for the top and bottom 25% of builders with land costs.

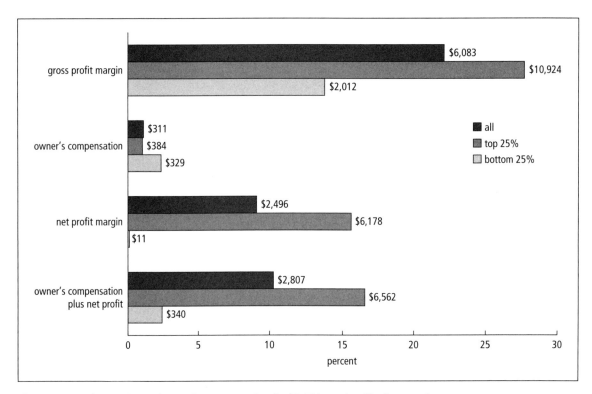

Figure 2.2 Profit margins and owner's compensation (in $1,000s and as % of revenue)

Table 2.5 Top and bottom 25%

	Top 25%	All	Bottom 25%
Gross profit margin	27.7%	22.1%	13.8%
Net profit margin	15.6%	9.1%	0.1%
Current ratio	1.60 to 1	1.56 to 1	1.19 to 1
Debt-to-equity ratio	1.59 to 1	2.44 to 2	3.22 to 1
Return on assets	24.8%	12.9%	0.05%
Return on equity	64.1%	44.5%	0.23%

3

Builders Without Land Costs

Respondents who build exclusively on land owned by their customers—*custom builders*—reported average revenues in 2006 of $4.9 million, average cost of goods sold of $4.1 million, and $773,000 in gross profit. Their gross profit margin was 15.9%. Cost of goods sold consumed 84.1% of revenue (table 3.1).

Owner's compensation for custom builders averaged 2.8% of revenue, more than twice both the overall average (1.3%) and the average for builders with land costs (1.1%). With higher-than-average general and administrative expenses as well (6.7% of revenue), operating expenses for custom builders were, on average, 11.5% of revenue (table 3.2).

After subtracting operating expenses, *builders without land costs* earned, on average, $214,000 in net profits, or 4.4% of total revenue (fig. 3.1).

As shown in table 3.3, builders without land costs held an average of $1.9 million in total assets, including $1 million in construction work in progress and $387,000 in cash. On the liabilities side, they held an average of $216,000 in construction loans and $680,000 in additional current liabilities. All liabilities combined averaged $1.3 million (67% of assets). Owner's equity averaged $615,000 (33% of assets).

The average current ratio for builders without land costs was 1.85 to 1. The debt-to-equity ratio was 2.03 to 1. Return on assets was 11.5% and return on equity was 34.8% (table 3.4).

Table 3.1 Gross profit

	Average (in $1,000s)	Share of revenue (%)
Revenue	4,865	100.0
Cost of goods sold		
Land costs	0	0.0
Direct costs: single family	2,958	60.8
Direct costs: multifamily, remodeling, light commercial/industrial	881	18.1
Indirect construction costs	233	4.8
Other costs	20	0.4
Total cost of goods sold	4,092	84.1
Gross profit	**773**	**15.9**

Builders Without Land Costs: Top and Bottom 25%

The top 25% of builders without land costs (measured by net profit margins) reported average revenue of $6.3 million, with 79.2% allocated to the cost of goods sold. Their average gross profit was $1.3 million, a 20.8% gross margin. After accounting for average operating expenses of $670,000, their net profit margin was 10.1%. Owner's compensation was 1.6% of total revenue (fig. 3.2).

Among those whose net profit margins were in the bottom 25%, average revenue was $3.6 million. The average cost of goods sold was $3.2 million, resulting in a gross profit margin of 12.3%. Operating expenses accounted for 14.3% of revenue, with owner's compensation consuming 4.1% of revenue. As a result, these builders had a negative average net profit margin of −2% (table 3.5).

Table 3.2 Net profit

	Average (in $1,000s)	Share of revenue (%)
Gross profit	773	15.9
Operating expenses		
Financing expenses	24	0.5
Sales & marketing expenses	74	1.5
General & administrative expenses	325	6.7
Owner's compensation	136	2.8
Total operating expenses	559	11.5
Net profit	**214**	**4.4**

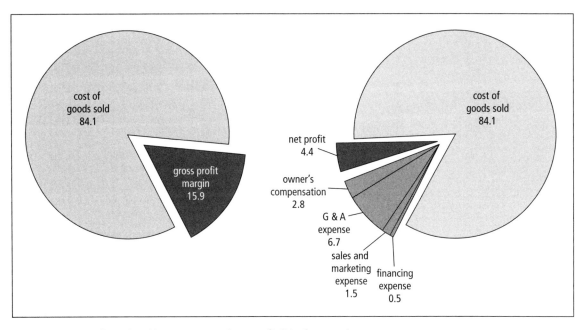

Figure 3.1 Cost of goods sold, expenses, and net profit (% of revenue)

Table 3.3 Balance sheet

	Average (in $1,000s)	Share of total (%)
Assets		
Current assets		
Cash	387	20.8
Construction work in progress	1,030	55.2
Other current assets	241	12.9
Total current assets	1,658	88.9
Other assets	208	11.1
Total assets	**1,865**	**100**
Median total assets	558	
Liabilities		
Current liabilities	680	36.5
Construction loans	216	11.5
Total current liabilities	896	48.0
Other liabilities	354	19.0
Total liabilities	**1,250**	**67.0**
Owner's equity	**615**	**33**
Median owner's equity	150	

Table 3.4 Financial ratios

Current ratio	1.85 to 1
Debt-to-equity ratio	2.03 to 1
Return on assets	11.5%
Return on equity	34.8%

Builders without land costs in the top 25% had an average of $3.2 million in total assets. With liabilities averaging $1.2 million, their average equity was $2 million.

Builders without land costs with the 25% lowest net profit margins reported average total assets of $1.9 million, liabilities of $1.8 million, and equity of $108,000 (Appendix I). Table 3.5 summarizes important statistics from the income statement and balance sheet for the top and bottom 25% of builders with land costs.

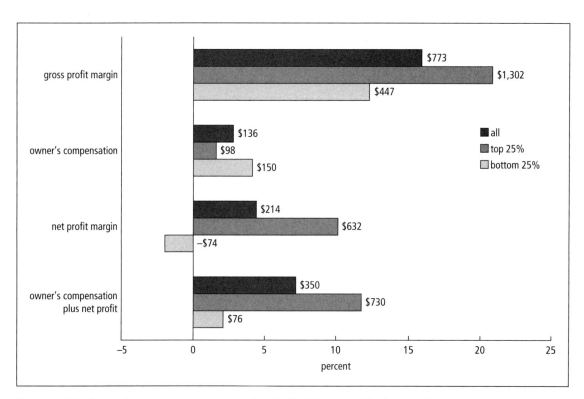

Figure 3.2 Profit margins and owner's compensation (in $1,000s and as % of revenue)

Table 3.5 Top and bottom 25%

	Top 25%	All	Bottom 25%
Gross profit margin	20.8%	15.9%	12.3%
Net profit margin	10.1%	4.4%	−2%
Current ratio	4.60 to 1	1.85 to 1	1.19 to 1
Debt-to-equity ratio	0.61 to 1	2.03 to 1	16.9 to 1
Return on assets	19.6%	11.5%	−3.8%
Return on equity	31.5%	34.8%	−68.5%

4

Combination Builders

Average revenue among builders who build on land they develop or purchase as well as on land their customers own was $13.7 million, roughly the midpoint between the $27.6 million in revenues for builders with land costs and the $4.9 million for builders without land costs. Of that amount, 82.1% paid for the cost of goods sold, leaving *combination builders* with a gross profit margin of 17.9% (table 4.1).

Table 4.2 shows the operating expenses for combination builders averaged $1.8 million, or 13.1% of revenue, higher than that of builders with land costs (13%) and builders without land costs (11.5%).

After subtracting operating expenses, combination builders had an average net profit of $661,000, a 4.8% net profit margin (fig. 4.1).

Combination builders had average total assets of $10.9 million, including $7.7 million in construction work in progress and $354,000 in cash. On the liabilities side, they had an average of $5.9 million in construction loans and $2.1 million in additional current liabilities. In all, as shown in table 4.3, liabilities averaged $8.7 million (80% of assets) and owner's equity averaged $2.2 million (20% of assets).

These builders averaged a current ratio of 1.17 to 1 and a debt-to-equity ratio of 3.94 to 1. Return on assets was 6.1% and return on equity was 30% (table 4.4).

Table 4.1 Gross profit

	Average (in $1,000s)	Share of revenue (%)
Revenue	13,731	100.0
Cost of goods sold		
Land costs	2,076	15.1
Direct costs: single family	7,725	56.3
Direct costs: multifamily, remodeling, light commercial/industrial	786	5.8
Indirect construction costs	438	3.2
Other costs	247	1.8
Total cost of goods sold	11,272	82.1
Gross profit	**2,459**	**17.9**

Top and Bottom 25% of Combination Builders

Among builders who construct homes both on land they develop or purchase and also on their customers' land, the top 25% reported $20.2 million in average revenue, $15.8 million in cost of goods sold, and gross profit of $4.4 million. Therefore, their gross margin was 21.6%. After subtracting operating expenses of $2.3 million, this group earned $2.1 million in net profit (fig. 4.2).

Combination builders with profit margins in the lowest 25% among their peers averaged $12.9 million in revenue and $11.4 million in cost of goods sold, for an average gross profit of $1.4 million. These builders spent more than they earned—an average of $1.6 million on operating expenses—so they had a negative net profit margin of −1.5%.

Table 4.2 Net profit

	Average (in $1,000s)	Share of revenue (%)
Gross profit	2,459	17.9
Operating expenses		
Financing expenses	327	2.4
Sales & marketing expenses	573	4.2
General & administrative expenses	694	5.1
Owner's compensation	203	1.5
Total operating expenses	1,798	13.1
Net profit	**661**	**4.8**

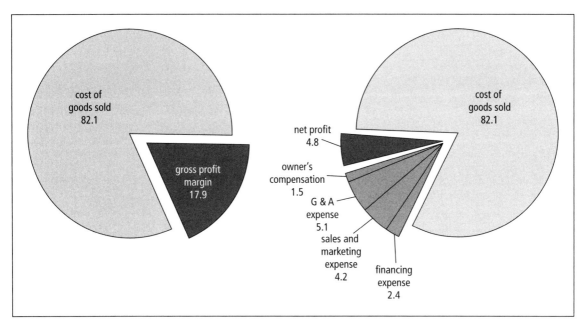

Figure 4.1 Cost of goods sold, expenses, and net profit (% of revenue)

Table 4.3 Balance sheet

	Average (in $1,000s)	Share of total (%)
Assets		
Current assets		
Cash	354	3.3
Construction work in progress	7,694	70.7
Other current assets	1,270	11.7
Total current assets	9,318	85.6
Other assets	1,569	14.4
Total Assets	**10,888**	**100**
Median total assets	3,327	
Liabilities		
Current liabilities	2,058	18.9
Construction loans	5,883	54
Total current liabilities	7,941	72.9
Other liabilities	743	6.8
Total liabilities	**8,684**	**79.8**
Owner's equity	**2,203**	**20.2**
Median owner's equity	393	

Table 4.4 Financial ratios

Current ratio	1.17 to 1
Debt-to-equity ratio	3.94 to 1
Return on assets	6.1%
Return on equity	30%

The top 25% of combination builders had average total assets of $13.9 million. With average total liabilities of $10.3 million, these builders had average equity of $3.6 million.

Combination builders with profit margins in the bottom 25% among their peers reported total assets of $14.5 million, liabilities of $12.3 million, and average equity of $2.2 million (Appendix I). Table 4.5 summarizes important statistics from the income statement and balance sheet for the top and bottom 25% of combination builders.

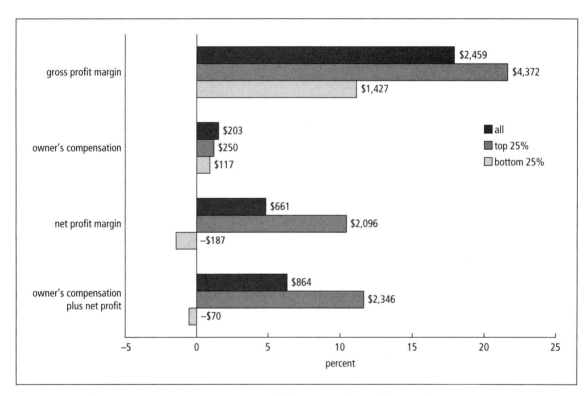

Figure 4.2 Profit margins and owner's compensation (in $1,000s and as % of revenue)

Table 4.5 Top and bottom 25%

	Top 25%	All	Bottom 25%
Gross profit margin	21.6%	17.9%	11.1%
Net profit margin	10.4%	4.8%	−1.5%
Current ratio	1.40 to 1	1.17 to 1	1.13 to 1
Debt-to-equity ratio	2.85 to 1	3.94 to 1	5.57 to 1
Return on assets	15%	6.1%	−1.3%
Return on equity	57.6%	30.0%	−8.5%

5

Small-Volume Builders

As shown in table 5.1, small-volume builders had average revenue of $4.3 million, $3.6 million in cost of goods sold, and gross profit of $726,000 (16.9% gross profit margin).

Operating expenses among small-volume builders averaged $570,000, or 13.3% of revenue (table 5.2).

After subtracting operating expenses, these builders had an average net profit of $156,000, or 3.6% of revenue (fig. 5.1).

Small-volume builders held average total assets of $2.8 million, including $1.9 million in construction work in progress and $302,000 in cash. On the liabilities side, they had an average of $1.2 million in construction loans and $776,000 in additional current liabilities. In all, this group's average equity was $535,000 (table 5.3).

These builders averaged a current ratio of 1.25 to 1 and a debt-to-equity ratio of 4.32 to 1. Return on assets was 5.5% and return on equity was 29.2% (table 5.4).

Small-Volume Builders With Land Costs

Small-volume builders who build on land they develop or purchase had average revenue of $4.2 million, cost of goods sold of $3.3 million, and a gross profit of $894,000, or 21.4% of revenue (table 5.5). Their operating expenses averaged $681,000, 16.3% of their revenue (table 5.6). After subtracting operating expenses from gross profit,

Table 5.1 Gross profit

	Average (in $1,000s)	Share of revenue (%)
Revenue	4,288	100.0
Cost of goods sold		
Land costs	365	8.5
Direct costs: single-family	2,625	61.2
Direct costs: multifamily, remodeling, light commercial/industrial	365	8.5
Indirect construction costs	159	3.7
Other costs	48	1.1
Total cost of goods sold	3,562	83.1
Gross profit	**726**	**16.9**

Table 5.2 Net profit

	Average (in $1,000s)	Share of revenue (%)
Gross profit	726	16.9
Operating expenses		
Financing expenses	74	1.7
Sales & marketing expenses	116	2.7
General & administrative expenses	249	5.8
Owner's compensation	132	3.1
Total operating expenses	570	13.3
Net profit	**156**	**3.6**

these builders had an average net profit of $213,000, or 5.1% of revenue (fig. 5.2).

Small-volume builders with land costs had $4.1 million in assets, including $3.1 million in construction work in progress and $358,000 in cash. They had $2.4 million in construction loans, $589,000 in additional current liabilities, and $748,000 in owner's equity (table 5.7).

These builders' current ratio averaged 1.28; their average debt-to-equity ratio was 4.43; return on assets was 5.2%; and return on equity was 28.5% (table 5.8).

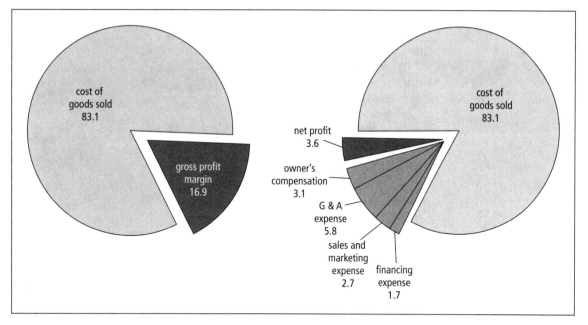

Figure 5.1 Small-volume builders: cost of goods sold, expenses, and net profit (% of revenue)

Table 5.3 Balance sheet

	Average (in $1,000s)	Share of total (%)
Assets		
Current assets		
Cash	302	10.6
Construction work in progress	1,853	65.1
Other current assets	352	12.4
Total current assets	2,507	88.1
Other assets	337	11.8
Total assets	**2,845**	**100.0**
Median total assets	1,622	
Liabilities		
Current liabilities	776	27.3
Construction loans	1,232	43.3
Total current liabilities	2,008	70.6
Other liabilities	301	10.6
Total liabilities	**2,309**	**81.2**
Owner's Equity	**535**	**18.8**
Median owner's equity	197	

Table 5.4 Financial ratios

Current ratio	1.25 to 1
Debt-to-equity ratio	4.32 to 1
Return on assets	5.5%
Return on equity	29.2%

Table 5.5 Gross profit (with land costs)

	Average (in $1,000s)	Share of revenue (%)
Revenue	4,168	100.0
Cost of goods sold		
Land costs	676	16.2
Direct costs: single family	2,313	55.5
Direct costs: multifamily, remodeling, light commercial/industrial	96	2.3
Indirect construction costs	124	3.0
Other costs	64	1.5
Total cost of goods sold	3,274	78.6
Gross profit	**894**	**21.4**

Table 5.6 Net profit (with land costs)

	Average (in $1,000s)	Share of revenue (%)
Gross profit	894	21.4
Operating expenses		
Financing expenses	141	3.4
Sales & marketing expenses	199	4.8
General & administrative expenses	197	4.7
Owner's compensation	143	3.4
Total operating expenses	681	16.3
Net profit	**213**	**5.1**

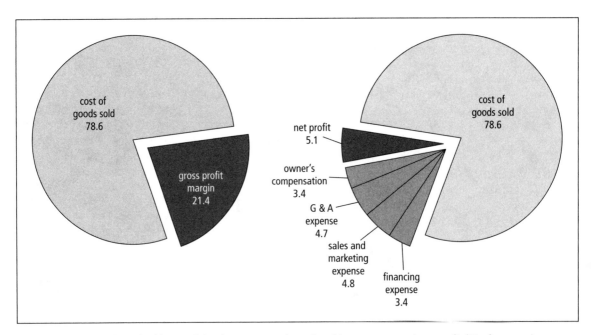

Figure 5.2 Small-volume builders with land costs: cost of goods sold, expenses, and net profit (% of revenue)

Table 5.7 Balance sheet (with land costs)

	Average (in $1,000s)	Share of total (%)
Assets		
Current Assets		
Cash	358	8.8
Construction work in progress	3,062	75.5
Other current assets	361	8.9
Total current assets	3,781	93.2
Other assets	277	6.8
Total assets	**4,058**	**100**
Median total assets	2,677	
Liabilities		
Current liabilities	589	14.5
Construction loans	2,359	58.1
Total current liabilities	2,948	72.6
Other liabilities	363	8.9
Total liabilities	**3,311**	**81.6**
Owner's equity	**748**	**18.4**
Median owner's equity	286	

Table 5.8 Financial ratios (with land costs)

Current ratio	1.28 to 1
Debt-to-equity ratio	4.43 to 1
Return on assets	5.2%
Return on equity	28.5%

Small-Volume Combination Builders

Small-volume builders who build both on land they purchase and/or develop as well as on their customers' land had average revenue of $4.5 million, with $3.8 million in cost of goods sold and gross profit of $719,000, a 15.9% gross profit margin (table 5.9). This group's operating expenses averaged $580,000, 12.8% of their revenue (table 5.10). After subtracting operating expenses from gross profit, small-volume combination builders had average net profit of $139,000, or 3.1% of revenue (fig. 5.3).

Small-volume combination builders held, on average, $219,000 in cash, $1.8 million in construction work in progress, and $1 million in other assets. They had $1.1 million in construction loans, $1 million in additional current liabilities, and $533,000 in owner's equity (table 5.11).

These builders averaged a current ratio of 1.16 to 1 and a debt-to-equity ratio of 4.57 to 1. Return on assets was 4.7% and return on equity was 26.1% (table 5.12).

Table 5.9 Gross profit (small-volume combination builders)

	Average (in $1,000s)	Share of revenue (%)
Revenue	4,536	100.0
Cost of goods sold		
Land costs	349	7.7
Direct costs: single family	2,832	62.4
Direct costs: multifamily, remodeling,		
light commercial/industrial	422	9.3
Indirect construction costs	153	3.4
Other costs	61	1.3
Total cost of goods sold	3,817	84.1
Gross profit	**719**	**15.9**

Table 5.10 Net profit (small-volume combination builders)

	Average (in $1,000s)	Share of revenue (%)
Gross profit	719	15.9
Operating expenses		
Financing expenses	71	1.6
Sales & marketing expenses	102	2.2
General & administrative expenses	278	6.1
Owner's compensation	129	2.8
Total operating expenses	580	12.8
Net profit	**139**	**3.1**

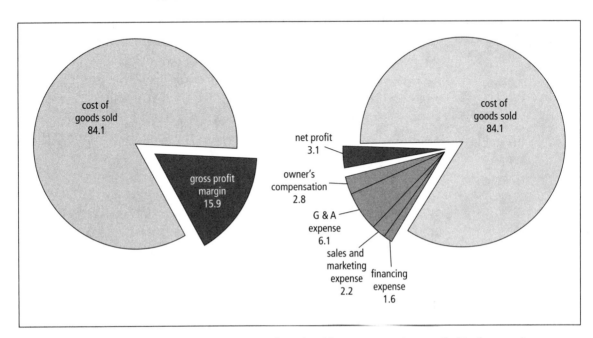

Figure 5.3 Small-volume combination builders: cost of goods sold, expenses, and net profit (% of revenue)

Table 5.11 Balance sheet (small-volume combination builders)

	Average (in $1,000s)	Share of total (%)
Assets		
Current Assets		
Cash	219	7.4
Construction work in progress	1,759	59.3
Other current assets	505	17.0
Total current assets	2,483	83.7
Other assets	483	16.3
Total assets	**2,967**	**100.0**
Median total assets	2,085	
Liabilities		
Current liabilities	1,015	34.2
Construction loans	1,124	37.9
Total current liabilities	2,139	72.1
Other liabilities	295	9.9
Total liabilities	**2,434**	**82.0**
Owner's equity	**533**	**18.0**
Median owner's equity	157	

Table 5.12 Financial ratios (small-volume combination builders)

Current ratio	1.16 to 1
Debt-to-equity ratio	4.57 to 1
Return on assets	4.7%
Return on equity	26.1%

6

Production Builders

Average revenue among *production builders* was $41.6 million. Most of the revenue, $37.5 million, was from single-family home building. Production builders' total cost of goods sold was $32.8 million, or 78.7% of revenue, leaving a gross profit margin of 21.3% (table 6.1).

Operating expenses among production builders averaged $5.4 million, 12.9% of revenue (table 6.2).

Production builders' average net profits, after accounting for operating expenses, were $3.5 million in 2006. Their net profit margin was 8.4% (fig. 6.1).

Production builders had average assets of $30 million in 2006, including $22.8 million in construction work in progress. On the liabilities side, they had an average of $15.1 million in construction loans and $3.1 million in additional current liabilities. Owner's equity for production builders averaged $8.4 million (table 6.3).

These builders had an average current ratio of 1.47 to 1 and a debt-to-equity ratio of 2.59 to 1. Their return on assets was 11.7% and return on equity was 41.9% (table 6.4).

Production Builders With Land Costs

The average revenue among production builders who build on land they develop or purchase was $44 million, including $40.2 million from single-family home building. Their total cost of goods sold was

Table 6.1 Gross profit

	Average (in $1,000s)	Share of revenue (%)
Revenue	41,620	100.0
Cost of goods sold		
Land costs	7,015	16.9
Direct costs: single family	21,745	52.2
Direct costs: multifamily, remodeling, light commercial/industrial	1,598	3.9
Indirect construction costs	1,302	3.1
Other costs	1,099	2.6
Total cost of goods sold	32,758	78.7
Gross profit	**8,862**	**21.3**

$34.3 million, leaving an average gross profit of $9.7 million, or a 22.1% gross profit margin (table 6.5).

Operating expenses among production builders with land costs averaged $5.6 million, which represents 12.8% of revenue (table 6.6).

Average net profit for production builders with land costs, after accounting for operating expenses, was $4.1 million in 2006, a 9.3% net profit margin (fig. 6.2).

Total assets for production builders with land costs averaged $30.4 million, including $2 million in cash. An additional $23.3 million was construction work in progress. Average liabilities were $21.2 million and owner's equity was $9.1 million (table 6.7).

Table 6.2 Net profit

	Average (in $1,000s)	Share of revenue (%)
Gross profit	8,862	21.3
Operating expenses		
Financing expenses	1,085	2.6
Sales & marketing expenses	1,879	4.5
General & administrative expenses	1,978	4.8
Owner's compensation	417	1.0
Total operating expenses	5,358	12.9
Net profit	**3,504**	**8.4**

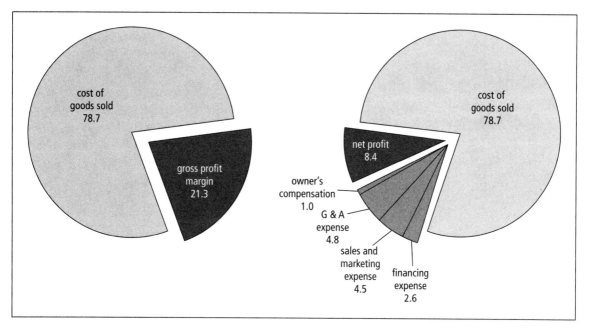

Figure 6.1 Cost of goods sold, expenses, and net profit (% of revenue)

Table 6.3 Balance sheet

	Average (in $1,000s)	Share of total (%)
Assets		
Current assets		
Cash	1,604	5.3
Construction work in progress	22,727	75.7
Other current assets	2,459	8.2
Total current assets	26,790	89.2
Other assets	3,231	10.8
Total assets	**30,022**	**100.0**
Median total assets	15,446	
Liabilities		
Current liabilities	3,103	10.3
Construction loans	15,066	50.2
Total current liabilities	18,169	60.5
Other liabilities	3,482	11.6
Total liabilities	**21,651**	**72.1**
Owner's equity	**8,370**	**27.9**
Median owner's equity	4,016	

Table 6.4 Financial ratios

Current ratio	1.47 to 1
Debt-to-equity ratio	2.59 to 1
Return on assets	11.7%
Return on equity	41.9%

Table 6.5 Gross profit (with land costs)

	Average (in $1,000s)	Share of revenue (%)
Revenue	44,027	100.0
Cost of goods sold		
Land costs	7,483	17.0
Direct costs: single-family	22,806	51.8
Direct costs: multifamily, remodeling, light commercial/industrial	1,359	3.1
Indirect construction costs	1,372	3.1
Other costs	1,273	2.9
Total cost of goods sold	34,292	77.9
Gross profit	**9,735**	**22.1**

Production builders with land costs had an average current ratio of 1.60 to 1 and a debt-to-equity ratio of 2.33 to 1. Their return on assets was 13.5% and return on equity was 44.9% (table 6.8).

Production Combination Builders

The average revenue among production builders who build both on land they purchase and/or develop and on land owned by their customers was $38.8 million. Their average cost of goods sold was $31.6 million and their average gross profit was $7.2 million, an 18.6% gross profit margin (table 6.9).

Operating expenses among production combination builders averaged $5.1 million, or 13.2% of revenue (table 6.10).

Table 6.6 Net profit (with land costs)

	Average (in $1,000s)	Share of revenue (%)
Gross profit	9,735	22.1
Operating expenses		
Financing expenses	1,157	2.6
Sales & marketing expenses	1,973	4.5
General & administrative expenses	2,074	4.7
Owner's compensation	429	1.0
Total operating expenses	5,632	12.8
Net profit	**4,102**	**9.3**

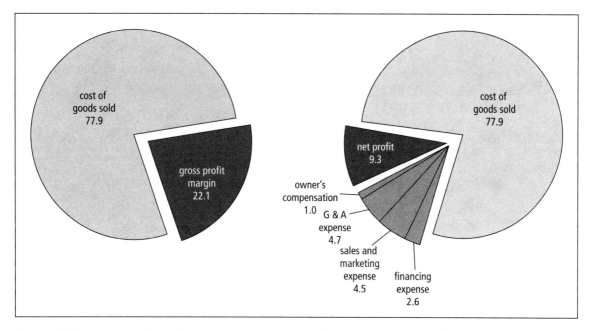

Figure 6.2 Production builders with land costs: cost of goods sold, expenses, and net profit (% of revenue)

Table 6.7 Balance sheet (with land costs)

	Average (in $1,000s)	Share of total (%)
Assets		
Current assets		
Cash	1,956	6.4
Construction work in progress	23,260	76.8
Other current assets	2,201	7.2
Total current assets	27,417	90.3
Other assets	2,937	9.7
Total assets	**30,354**	**100.0**
Median total assets	14,099	
Liabilities		
Current liabilities	2,628	8.6
Construction loans	14,514	47.9
Total current liabilities	17,142	56.4
Other liabilities	4,087	13.3
Total liabilities	**21,229**	**69.7**
Owner's equity	**9,126**	**30.3**
Median owner's equity	3,516	

Table 6.8 Financial ratios (with land costs)

Current ratio	1.60 to 1
Debt-to-equity ratio	2.33 to 1
Return on assets	13.5%
Return on equity	44.9%

Table 6.9 Gross profit (production combination builders)

	Average (in $1,000s)	Share of revenue (%)
Revenue	38,761	100.0
Cost of goods sold		
Land costs	6,779	17.5
Direct costs: single family	21,046	54.3
Direct costs: multifamily, remodeling, light commercial/industrial	1,777	4.6
Indirect construction costs	1,212	3.1
Other costs	752	1.9
Total cost of goods sold	31,567	81.4
Gross profit	**7,194**	**18.6**

Average net profit for production combination builders, after accounting for operating expenses, was $2.1 million in 2006—a 5.4% net profit margin (fig. 6.3).

Production combination builders held total average assets of $32.9 million, including $24.2 million in construction work in progress and $730,000 in cash. They had average liabilities of $19.1 million in construction loans and $6.9 million in other liabilities. Equity averaged $6.8 million (table 6.11).

Their current ratio was 1.18 to 1 and their debt-to-equity ratio was 3.81 to 1. Return on assets was 6.3% and return on equity was 30.4% (table 6.12).

Table 6.10 Net profit (production combination builders)

	Average (in $1,000s)	Share of revenue (%)
Gross profit	7,194	18.6
Operating expenses		
Financing expenses	1,023	2.6
Sales & marketing expenses	1,856	4.8
General & administrative expenses	1,827	4.7
Owner's compensation	407	1.1
Total operating expenses	5,112	13.2
Net profit	**2,082**	**5.4**

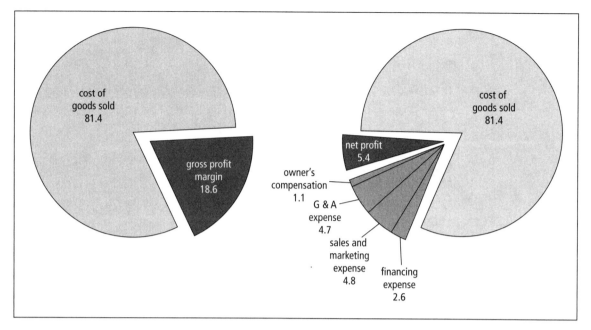

Figure 6.3 Production combination builders: cost of goods sold, expenses, and net profit (% of revenue)

Table 6.11 Balance sheet (production combination builders)

	Average (in $1,000s)	Share of total (%)
Assets		
Current assets		
Cash	730	2.2
Construction work in progress	24,180	73.5
Other current assets	3,396	10.3
Total current assets	28,306	86.0
Other assets	4,584	13.9
Total Assets	**32,889**	**100**
Median total assets	20,735	
Liabilities		
Current liabilities	4,955	15.1
Construction loans	19,103	58.1
Total current liabilities	24,058	73.1
Other liabilities	1,987	6.0
Total liabilities	**26,045**	**79.2**
Owner's equity	**6,844**	**20.8**
Median owner's equity	4,941	

Table 6.12 Financial ratios (production combination builders)

Current ratio	1.18 to 1
Debt-to-equity ratio	3.81 to 1
Return on assets	6.3%
Return on equity	30.4%

7

Builder Financial Performance by Region and Business Model

Builders in all regions earned most of their revenue from single-family home building in all regions (Appendix I). Single-family home building accounted for 95% of their revenue in the West, 87% in the South, 83% in the Northeast, and 80% in the Midwest.

Profits and Costs by Region

Land and direct construction costs were highest (as a percentage of revenue) in the West, where these expenses consumed, respectively, 17.2% and 58% of revenue. Land costs consumed 16.8% of revenues in the Midwest, 15.7% in the South, and 11.8% in the Northeast.[3]

Depending on region, operating expenses were 11%–14% of revenue. After accounting for all costs of goods sold, builders in the Northeast had an average gross profit margin of 23%; builders in the South, 22.8%; builders in the West, 20.2%; and builders in the Midwest, 16.4%. Net profit margins by region were: 11.7% in the Northeast, 8.6% in the South, 7.8% in the West, and 4% in the Midwest (fig. 7.1).

Comparing Types of Builders

The survey found significant differences in financial performance among builders with land costs, those without land costs, and combination builders (fig. 7.1). Interestingly, builders with land costs have the highest

---

[3] The Northeast region's average land costs are skewed downward by the presence of a significant number of custom builders ($0 land costs) in its sample set.

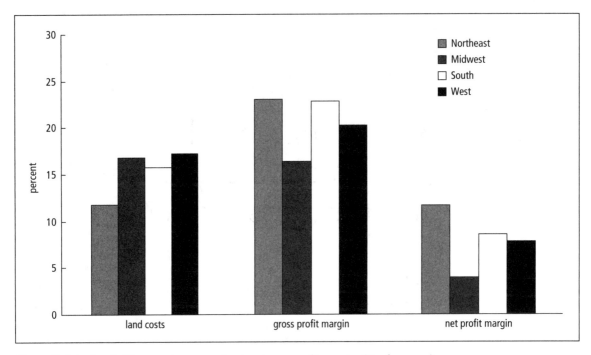

Figure 7.1 Regional differences in average land costs and profit margins (% of revenue)

gross profit margins, the lowest share of revenue going to owner's compensation, and the highest net profit margins.

Considering net profit margins and owner's compensation together, combination builders demonstrated the weakest performance among all three groups of builders. Their owner's compensation and net profit together totaled 6.3% of revenue. Builders with land costs showed the strongest performance with owner's compensation and net profit totaling 10.2%. Financial performance of builders without land costs was in the middle, with owner's compensation and net profits totaling 7.2% (fig. 7.2).

In terms of assets, builders who build only on land they develop or purchase held an average of $19.3 million in assets in 2006, including $14.8 million invested in construction work in progress. Total liabilities averaged $13.7 million, including $9.4 million in construction loans. As a result, builders with land costs had an average of $5.6 million in owner's equity (fig. 7.3).

Among builders who build exclusively on land their customers own, average assets were $1.9 million, including $387,000 in cash and $1 million in construction work in progress. This group of builders reported

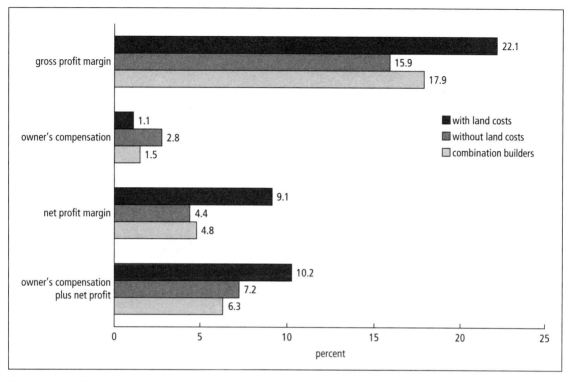

Figure 7.2 Profits and owner's compensation for three types of builders (% of revenue)

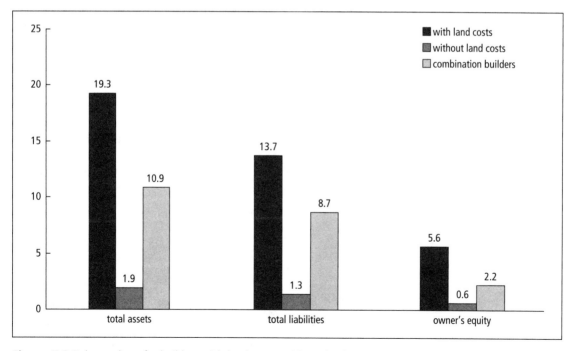

Figure 7.3 Balance sheet for builders with land costs, without land costs, and combination builders ($ averages in millions)

total liabilities of $1.3 million, and $680,000 in current liabilities. Their average equity was $615,000.

Combination builders reported assets averaging $10.9 million in 2006, roughly the midpoint between the amount held by builders with land costs and those without. With $8.7 million in liabilities, $5.9 million of which were in construction loans, combination builders had average owner's equity of $2.2 million.

8

Operations and Number of Years in Business

Eighty-six percent of survey respondents mainly built single-family homes. Thirty-six percent of respondents were mainly single-family production builders; 26% mainly built custom homes on their customers' land; and 24% built custom homes on their own land. Eight percent of respondents mainly did residential remodeling and rehabilitation and 2% mainly built multifamily condo and/or co-op units. One percent each of the respondents were land developers and multifamily builders of rental units (fig. 8.1).

Builders' main operations varied by region and total revenue. Forty-five percent of builders in the West were mainly single-family production builders, whereas 23% of builders in the Northeast were. Whether they built on their own lots or on customers' lots, 62% of builders who earned less than $2 million in revenue in 2006, compared with 22% of those who earned $10 million or more, said they mainly built single-family custom homes.

Eight percent of respondents said residential remodeling and/or rehabilitation was their main operation. Ten percent and 13%, respectively, of respondents in the Northeast and the Midwest said remodeling was their main operation. Remodeling also was the main operation for 18% of builders who earned less than $2 million, for 13% of builders who earned $2–$4.9 million, and for 3% of those who earned $5–$9.9 million. There were no builders who closed 10 or more homes in 2006 who said remodeling was their main operation.

Builders also were asked what share each of these operations accounted for in their business. Single-family production building accounted for, on average, 30% of the respondents' businesses; single-family custom building on the owner's land, 24%; and single-family custom building

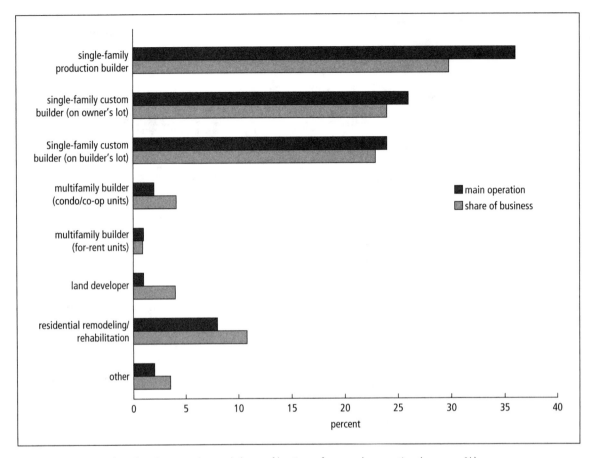

Figure 8.1 Respondents' main operation and share of business from each operation (average %)

on the builder's land, 23%. Residential remodeling/rehabilitation, on average, accounted for 11% of their businesses. Multifamily condominium building and land development each accounted for an average of 4% of the respondents' businesses.

By revenue source, single-family custom building (whether on the customer's or the builder's land) was least significant for builders earning $10 million or more; these activities represented an average of 23% of their businesses. In contrast, among builders with revenues of $2–$4.9 million, and $5–$9.9 million, custom building accounted for 62% of their businesses. For builders earning less than $2 million, custom building represented about 57% of their businesses and residential remodeling and/or rehabilitation 22%.

Overall, 35% of respondents were involved in residential remodeling and/or rehabilitation. Forty-one percent of builders with 10–25 closings, 14% of those with 26–99 closings, and 5% of those with 100 or more closings in 2006 said they did residential remodeling and rehabilitation (fig. 8.2).

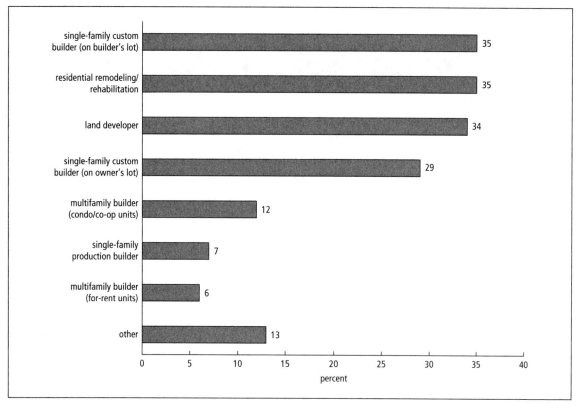

Figure 8.2 All other important operations (% of all respondents)

Constructing single-family custom homes on the builder's land was a secondary operation for 35% of respondents. Thirty-four percent and 29% of respondents, respectively, said that land development and single-family custom building on the customer's land were secondary operations.

Status of Firm's Operating Head

Seventy-three percent of respondents were owner-operators and 19% were sole owners of their companies. Only 6% of firms included in the survey were headed by a salaried executive (fig. 8.3).

Years in Business

Approximately half of respondents (51%) had been in residential construction for 20 years or longer and 29% had been in business for 11–19 years (fig. 8.4). For all respondents, the median number of years in business was 20. By geographic region, respondents from the Northeast had been

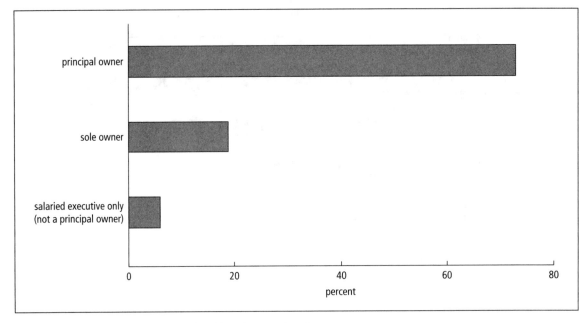

Figure 8.3 Status of firm's operating head (% of respondents)

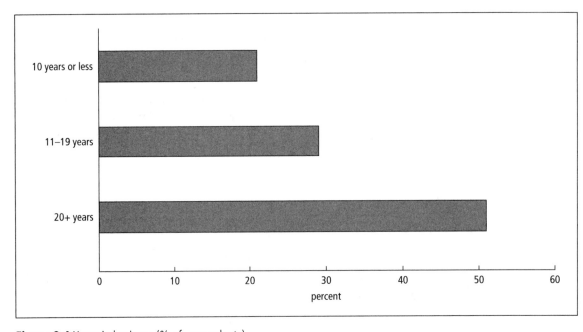

Figure 8.4 Years in business (% of respondents)

in business the longest—27 years on average. Builders in the Midwest had been in business for an average of 23 years, and those in the South and West, 19 years.

Builders with land costs had been in business for 21 years on average, slightly less than the 23-year average for builders without land costs. The data show a positive correlation of years in business with total revenue. Firms that earned $2–$4.9 million in 2006 had been in business an average of 19 years; those with revenue of $5–$9.9 million had existed for 20 years; and businesses with revenue topping $10 million had been in business an average of 23 years.

Units Closed: Presold, Speculative, or on Customers' Land

Respondents closed an average of 52 homes in 2006. They were asked to specify whether these homes were presold, built on speculation, or built on customers' land. On average, respondents closed 29 presold homes (57% of all the homes they closed), 18 speculative homes (35%), and 4 custom homes (9%), for an average of 52 homes closed.

Builders with land costs closed an average of 80 homes, 50 of which were presold and 30 speculative. The median number of homes these builders closed was 38. Builders without land costs built an average of 12 homes and a median of 3. Combination builders built an average of 42 homes, 6 of which were on land owned by their customers (fig. 8.5).

Units Closed: Sources of Land

The survey asked builders about the number of single-family units built on land that their firm developed, purchased, or which was customer-owned. Out of an average of 52 homes closed, 54% were built on land developed by the builder, 37% were built on land purchased by the builder (already developed), and 9% were built on the customers' land.

By region, 49% of homes built by respondents in the South were on land the builders purchased, compared with the Midwest and West, with 29% and 26%, respectively. In the Northeast, 21% of units closed were built on land owned by the customer, compared with 8% each in the South and Midwest, and 4% in the West.

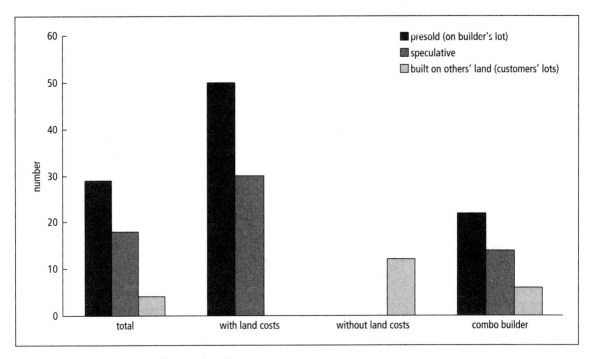

Figure 8.5 Average number of homes closed

Units Closed: Type of Construction

The vast majority of homes survey respondents built were stick built. Of 52 homes closed in 2006, 95% were stick built, 5% were panelized, and one was built with some "other" method of construction.

Regionally, all single-family homes survey respondents closed in the West were stick-built, as were 93% in the South, 94% in the Northeast, and 95% in the Midwest. About 6% of homes closed in the Northeast and South were panelized; about 5% of homes in the Midwest were constructed with panels.

Most builders with land costs use stick-built construction: Of the average of 80 homes this group closed, 95% were stick-built. These builders closed an average of 4 panelized homes, or 5% of the average total. Builders without land costs, on average, closed 10 stick-built (90%) and one panelized home (9%). Combination builders closed an average of 40 stick-built homes, one panelized home, and one using some "other" construction method.

9

Historical Perspective

NAHB has conducted the *Cost of Doing Business Study* 15 times since 1970. The survey focuses on builders' income statements and balance sheets to learn how builders handle their companies' finances.

The survey shows that the 2006 cost of goods sold accounted for 79.2% percent of total sales, slightly more than the 79.1% reported in 2004, but less than the 81.1% reported in 2002 (table 9.1).

The cost of sales category includes land costs, direct and indirect construction costs, and all other costs of goods sold.

The latest survey indicates that gross profit, at 20.8%, was barely below that in 2004, when it was 20.9%. Since the survey's inception, only 3 other years have seen higher gross profit margins: 1978 (23.9%), 1980 (22.8%), and 1991 (22%).

Total operating expenses in 2006 were 13.1% of total revenue, slightly higher than in 2004 (12.9%), despite declines in the average revenue shares of sales and marketing expenses and general and administrative expenses. Increased financing costs was the main reason for the increase in operating expenses. The cost of financing rose from 1.5%–2.5% between 2004 and 2006, whereas the share of revenue spent on owner's compensation in 2006 remained steady at 1.3%.

In the end, the net profit margin reported for 2006 was 7.7% of total revenue, below 2004 (8%), but still far ahead of 2002 (5.4%). The highest net profit margin ever reported in the *Cost of Doing Business Study* was 10% in 1991.

Table 9.1 Summary data from *Cost of Doing Business* studies, 1970–2006 (% of revenue)

Study*	Cost of goods sold	Gross profit	Finance	Sales and marketing	General & administrative	Owner's compensation†	Total operating expense	Net income before tax
2006	79.2%	20.8%	2.5%	4.4%	5%	1.3%	13.1%	7.7%
2004	79.1	20.9	1.5	4.7	5.4	1.3	12.9	8.0
2002	81.1	18.9	0.6	2.6	5.9	4.5	13.6	5.4
2000	80.1	19.9	2.2	5.7	3.9	1.8	13.5	6.3
1996	82.4	17.6	1.5	3.3	5.0	3.4	13.2	4.4
1993	79.4	20.6	1.9	4.0	5.1	5.0	16.0	4.6
1991	78	22	3.0	4.0	5.0		12.0	10
1989	79.1	20.9	5.6	5.2	4.8		15.6	5.3
1987	79.7	20.3	3.3	3.7	6.1		13.1	7.2
1985	81.7	18.3	3.9	3.3	7.6		14.8	3.5
1983‡	79.7	20.3	4.5	3.3	8.8		17.6	2.7
1980‡	77.2	22.8	2.0	2.5	9.4		16.9	5.9
1978	76.1	23.9	2.7	3.6	5.5		16.9	7.0
1975	84.1	15.9	2.8	2.3	7.5		11.6	4.3
1970	82.4	17.6	3.3	3.0	6.5		14.4	3.2

Source: NAHB

Note: The 1998 *Cost of Doing Business Study* does not appear in this table because the survey for that edition did not ask for an income statement breakdown.

*Beginning with the 1983 data the report titles used the year of publication rather than the year data were collected.

†Data was not collected prior to the 1993 study.

‡The values for 1980 and 1983 are medians.

Construction Cost Surveys

In addition to the *Cost of Doing Business Study* surveys, NAHB has surveyed builders regularly about construction costs. These surveys collect detailed information about the cost of components such as insulation, windows, plumbing, and land development. Table 9.2 summarizes the results.

The 2006 Construction Cost Survey found that the finished lot cost accounted for 24.5% of the sales price, down from 26% in 2004, but higher than in 2002, when it was 23.5%. Total construction cost, consisting of labor and materials, accounted for 48.1% of a home's sales price in 2006—the first time since 1982 that construction costs represented less than half of the home price.

Financing costs in 2006, at 2.4% of the sales price, were the highest since 1982, when they were 15%. Overhead, marketing costs, sales commissions, and profit accounted for 25% of the 2006 sales price, the highest percentage since the survey's inception. In 2006, profits were 11.2% of a home's sales price: above 2004 (9.8%) but below 2002 (12%).

Table 9.2 Cost breakdown of single family home (national)

	1949	1969	1982	1995	1998	2002	2004	2006
Sale price breakdown				% of total sale price				
Finished lot cost	11	21	24	24.4	23.6	23.5	26.0	24.5
Total construction cost	69	55	45	53.3	54.8	50.8	51.7	48.1
Financing cost	5	7	15	2	1.9	2.1	1.8	2.4
Other costs*	15	17	16	20.4	19.7	23.6	20.5	25
Overhead & general expenses				5.8	5.7	5.5	5.8	7
Marketing cost				2.2	1.4	2.4	1.9	2.5
Sales commission				3.3	3.4	3.7	3	4.3
Profit				9.1	9.2	12.0	9.8	11.2
Sale price	$9,500	$26,000	$70,000	$183,585	$226,680	$298,412	$373,349	$454,906

Source: NAHB Surveys of builder members
Note: 2002 data based on survey of builder members carried out in late 2002–early 2003.
*No breakdown of "other costs" available for 1949, 1969, and 1982.

Housing Giants

Professional Builder magazine also conducts an important annual *Housing Giants* study of the top 400 builders based on revenues (table 9.3).

The 2006 data show that materials costs accounted for 27% of home prices, the lowest percentage for all years reported. Raw land cost accounted for 9.5% of a home's sales price in 2006, roughly the same as in 2004 but higher than in 2000 (7%) and 2001 (7.2%). The aggregate cost for raw land, land improvements, improved lot costs, fees, and indirect construction costs accounted for 25.4% of the home price, about the same as in 2004 (25.2%) but higher than in 2001 (23.1%). Profit as a percentage of sales price was less in 2006 (10.2%) than in 2004 (10.9%), but significantly higher than in 1995 (6%).

Public Firms' Financial Reports

The financial reports of publicly traded firms offer another perspective on profitability in the construction industry. The pretax profit margin was on an upward trend for all companies from 1998 to 2004. However, in 2006, the group had the lowest combined pretax profit margin since 2001 (9.9%). Among public firms, NVR and Toll Brothers consistently have earned the highest pretax profit margins for 2004–06 (table 9.4).

Table 9.3 Housing giants' average home price breakdown (expenses as a percentage of the average unit sales price)

	1995	1999	2000	2001	2004	2006
Land/entitlement/financing expenses						
Raw land	10.7	7.6	7.0	7.2	9.4	9.5
Land improvements	8.6	5.5	5.6	5.3	4	4.3
Improved lot costs	na	6.7	7.2	7.2	7.6	7
Fees (permits, impact fees, etc.)	2.8	2.2	2.2	2.1	1.9	1.9
Financing costs	3.1	3.3	2.9	2.8	2.2	2.7
Hard costs						
Materials	29.7	32	31.8	30.2	27.6	27
Construction labor	19.3	20.3	20.7	21.8	22.4	21.5
Indirect construction costs*	3.6	1.6	1.5	1.3	2.3	2.7
Sales/marketing expenses						
Advertising	1.6	1.2	1.2	1.2	1.1	1.1
Marketing	1.4	1.2	1.2	1.2	0.9	1.5
Model merchandising	1.2	0.9	0.8	0.9	0.9	0.9
Sales commissions	2.8	2.9	2.9	3	2.8	3
Overhead/profit/miscellaneous						
Overhead expenses (salaries, office, etc.)	5.9	6	6.5	6.4	5.4	5.9
Profit	6	7.9	7.8	8.6	10.9	10.2
Miscellaneous	3.4	0.6	0.7	0.8	0.9	0.7

Source: *Professional Builder* Giant 400. Compiled by NAHB Economics.

Note: 2004 and 2006 data do not include results for the top 5 builders.

*Indirect construction costs were called "landscaping/community amenities" in previous reports.

Table 9.4 Publicly traded builders' revenues and profits

	2006 ($ millions)			2005 ($ millions)			2004 ($ millions)		
	Revenue	Pretax profit	After-tax profit	Revenue	Pretax profit	After-tax profit	Revenue	Pretax profit	After-tax profit
Lennar	15,623	943	594	13,305	2,160	1,355	10,505	1,519	946
D. R. Horton	14,761	1,879	1,233	13,629	2,273	1,471	10,841	1,583	975
Pulte	13,975	1,010	687	14,975	2,299	1,492	11,711	1,601	998
Centex	12,852	1,872	1,289	9,934	1,378	1,011	9,756	1,045	828
KB Homes	10,984	698	482	9,410	1,290	824	7,053	718	237
Hovnanian Enterprises	6,148	233	150	5,348	781	472	4,160	550	349
Toll Brothers	6,123	1,127	687	5,793	1,323	806	3,893	647	409
NVR	6,036	963	587	5,178	1,144	698	4,328	872	523
Beazer	5,462	613	389	4,995	499	263	3,907	387	236
Ryland	4,757	567	360	4,818	721	447	3,952	521	321
MDC Holdings	4,651	333	214	4,792	809	506	4,009	637	391
Standard Pacific	3,964	194	124	4,010	711	441	3,357	513	316
Meritage Homes	3,461	364	225	3,001	416	256	2,040	225	139
Technical Olympic USA	2,637	244	201	2,509	345	218	2,135	190	120
Total	**111,434**	**11,040**	**7,222**	**101,697**	**16,149**	**10,260**	**81,647**	**11,008**	**6,788**

Table 9.5 Publicly traded builders' pretax profit margins (%)

	2006	2005	2004	2003	2002	2001	2000	1999	1998
Lennar	6.0	16.2	14.5	13.5	12.1	11.4	8.0	9.2	9.9
D. R. Horton	12.7	16.7	14.6	11.5	9.6	9.2	8.5	8.4	7.3
Pulte	7.2	15.4	13.7	11.1	9.8	9.1	8.4	7.6	5.8
Centex	14.6	13.9	10.7	11.1	8.9	8.1	6.5	6.9	7.1
KB Homes	6.4	13.7	10.2	9.5	9.3	7.1	7.6	5.9	6.0
Hovnanian Enterprises	3.8	14.6	13.2	12.9	8.9	6.1	4.6	5.4	4.4
Toll Brothers	18.4	22.8	16.6	14.8	14.9	15.2	12.7	10.9	11.1
NVR	16.0	22.1	20.1	18.9	17.1	15.1	10.0	9.2	7.1
Beazer	11.2	10.0	9.9	9.0	7.6	6.8	4.6	4.3	3.8
Ryland	11.9	15.0	13.2	11.5	10.7	7.9	5.8	5.4	4.2
MDC Holdings	7.2	16.9	15.9	11.9	11.8	12.0	11.6	9.4	6.7
Standard Pacific	4.9	17.7	15.3	14.2	10.3	13.3	12.6	9.5	10.5
Meritage Homes	10.5	13.9	11.0	10.3	10.2	11.2	11.0	9.4	11.7
Technical Olympic USA	9.3	13.8	8.9	7.7	7.6	9.8	6.7	5.9	4.9
	9.9	**15.9**	**13.6**	**12.0**	**10.5**	**9.8**	**8.1**	**7.6**	**7.0**

Source: Form 10-K annual reports, U.S. Securities and Exchange Commission

10

Financial Management for Home Builders in a Changing Housing Market

By Steven W. Hays, Sr., CPA

Builders in markets in the midst of a slowdown should take the following actions to minimize the economic impact on their businesses:

- control fixed general and administrative expenses
- develop and closely monitor budgets for other fixed expenses and capital items
- control and manage the number of speculative and display homes carried
- closely monitor the relationship between staffing and sales volume
- manage and reduce direct construction costs

Control Fixed General and Administrative Expenses

General and administrative expenses are the costs of running your office, such as company officer and other salaries, related payroll taxes and fringe benefits, rent, office supplies, training, insurance, travel, entertainment, and professional fees. Since these expenses remain the same regardless of the number of houses closed, they can consume an increasing percentage of profits. These expenses should be monitored and, if possible, reduced. Employees should be cross-trained to absorb personnel losses, and businesses should carefully assess their personnel resources before hiring new staff.

Monitor the number of employees by job function, based on your projected sales volume. Anticipated closings must be able to support the number of superintendents, estimators, general laborers, general and administrative staff, and subcontractors. While 80 closings might warrant having two superintendents, closing volume of 40 or 50 units might not.

Develop and Closely Monitor Budgets for Other Fixed Expenses and Capital Items

Establish budgets for other fixed costs such as advertising, promotion, and donations. For example, if a builder's total budget for advertising is 1% of sales, all expenses of this type, such as print and media ads, should be monitored during the year to ensure that they don't exceed the budget.

In addition, establish a prioritized budget for adding fixed assets and perform a cost-benefit analysis before purchasing items. Rather than buying new model home furnishings, use existing items from prior models.

Manage and Control the Number of Speculative and Display Homes

As a market slows, adequately planning and managing the number of spec and model homes included in inventory becomes increasingly important. Therefore, build according to your anticipated closing volume as sitting inventory will negatively impact financing and model home costs.

Manage and Reduce Direct Construction Costs

Slower cycles are an especially good time to review direct construction costs. Even a small reduction in each home's cost can add significantly to the bottom line. In particular, value engineering can help determine what features in the base model can be replaced by less costly items that will not detract from the consumer appeal of the product. The best places to go for ideas to reduce costs or to discover possible design alternatives are your subcontractors and suppliers. Ideas that can be duplicated across your homes will multiply your savings and add profits to your bottom line.

Steven W. Hays, Sr., CPA, is partner-in-charge of the Home Builders Services Group of RubinBrown LLP CPAs, in St. Louis, Missouri. RubinBrown serves more than 35 Home Builder groups in the Midwest and Florida. Contact Steve at 314-290-3336, or e-mail steve.hays@rubinbrown.com.

11

The Balance Sheet: A Tool for Measuring, Managing Risk

By Ron Robichaud

T he balance sheet is a useful tool for a builder to assess the value of his or her company and how everyday management decisions impact its value at a given time. By regularly consulting their balance sheets, builders can manage and measure risk, determine if assets are being effectively used, and, perhaps most importantly, justify their risk position as entrepreneurs. However, few builders actually use the balance sheet except as their lenders require it.

Most home builders not only manage their company's operations, they are the largest, if not the only, shareholders. Moreover, their companies often are the source of the home builder's net worth. Therefore, it is incumbent on a builder to take the posture of an investor, as well as an operator. The scorecard for doing this is the balance sheet.

The investor's objective is twofold: first, to place an investment where it will generate the greatest return; and second, to measure financial performance in light of the investment's return. As a matter of fact, the most widely used measurement tools for large builders in evaluating their division's performance are those that calculate return on average net invested assets (RONA). While called by various names, all similar tools take the investor posture by assessing where to place capital in order to generate the greatest return with the least risk.

Large builders define net invested assets as the capital they have invested in the company, without distinguishing between debt and equity. Arriving at the number depends on the structure of the balance sheet, but in most cases it is calculated by deducting cash, accruals, payables, and customer deposits from a company's total assets. Next, average net invested assets over the course of the year are deducted. Since that information is

53

not readily available to many private builders, these builders can average beginning-of-the-year numbers with the year-end numbers. Finally, the return is calculated by dividing the earnings before interest and taxes (EBIT) by the average net assets.

Table 11.1 compares company A and company B. Both companies have $20 million in revenues, 27% gross margin, and $2.2 million of EBIT, or 11% of revenues. Three important conclusions can be drawn from the two balance sheets.

1. **The balance sheet is critical to calculating the "asset turnover" ratio.** This ratio helps builders understand the impact that cycle time has on revenues, pricing strategies, and ultimately the value of the company. It reveals the amount of sales generated for every dollar worth of assets.

Table 11.1 Balance sheet comparison

	$1,000s	
	A	B
Assets		
Cash	500	500
Receivables	0	0
Deposits on land	750	750
Work in process		
Houses	4,000	7,000
Land	2,500	4,500
Furniture & equipment (net)	250	250
Total assets	**8,000**	**13,000**
Liabilities		
Accounts payable	1,400	2,500
Customer deposits	500	500
Reserve for warranty	60	60
Debt	4,530	8,430
Total liabilities	**6,490**	**11,490**
Equity	1,510	1,510
Total liabilities & equity	**8,000**	**13,000**
Invested assets		
Assets	8,000	13,000
Less cash	(500)	(500)
Less accounts payable	(1,400)	(2,500)
Less customer deposits	(500)	(500)
Invested assets	**5,600**	**9,500**
RONA	39%	23%

The asset turnover for each company can be determined by dividing revenue ($20 million) by total liabilities and equity ($8 million for A and $13 million for B). The resulting turnover rate measures how quickly a firm is using its assets to build houses and, thus, generate revenue. company A's assets are being turned, or used, approximately 2.5 times a year, whereas company B's assets are being turned approximately 1.5 times a year. The construction cycle for company A appears to be much shorter than for company B because A turns over its assets more times per period. This means company A is using its assets much more efficiently than B, resulting in a greater return. Company A is producing and selling more houses in a year. Meanwhile, company B has its capital tied up in production longer. In order to be viable with this greater cycle time, company B needs to charge, and must be able to get, a higher sales price for its houses.

2. **The balance sheet helps calculate the risk associated with a company.** In general, a company is considered to have greater risk associated with it when large amounts of debt are used to finance projects. Using significant amounts of debt for financing is risky if there is uncertainty about a company's ability to repay it. The balance sheet not only helps builders visualize how much debt a company is using for leverage, but also reveals whether that company has debt coverage. The balance sheet illustrates how likely a company is to pay back its debt. Comparing debt with equity and cash flow on the balance sheet reveals whether a company can repay its debts. EBIT can represent a company's cash flow because these earnings are available to pay off debt.

   Company A's balance sheet contains $4,530,000 of debt—approximately 3 times the company's equity and twice its cash flow. For a private home builder, this is a relatively moderate risk position. However, company B's balance sheet shows $8,430,000 of debt, 5.6 times equity and almost 4 times cash flow. This is a very high-risk profile; it indicates that the company is highly vulnerable to market volatility. Debt should not be significantly higher than equity and/or cash flow because of the risk of not being able to pay back debt. Furthermore, if risk is measured by the ability to pay back debt from equity and/or cash flow, then builders who do not pay attention to the balance sheet may increase their risk position without being aware of the magnitude of the risk or its impact on the value of their companies.

3. **The balance sheet helps calculate expected return on investment.** Using the balance sheet to measure returns is important not only in

managing a company, but in valuing that company as a potential investment. An investor, or someone who wants to buy a company, will set his or her targeted return based on how they view the risk associated with a purchase and what kind of return could be generated from alternative uses of the capital.

Assuming a buyer requires a 27% return in order to justify an investment (this return would be within previously stated range for large builders), company A's 39% return would be very attractive. When the return earned by the company is actually higher than the buyer's target, the buyer will pay a premium, or an amount over the book value, for assets. This premium is a profit for the seller, but is allocated to the assets by the buyer after purchase. In this transaction, the book value of the assets is increased by the amount the buyer pays for the assets over their book value at the time of purchase, resulting in a decreased return. For this reason, a buyer must calculate how much of a premium he or she can pay for an investment and still get the targeted return.

Company B would be an unattractive investment because its 23% return is below the buyer's target rate. This investment also would not justify a premium.

The balance sheet is an important, and often overlooked, tool in business management. Business owners can, and should, use the balance sheet for more than neatly organizing assets, liabilities, and equity. Regularly examine your company's balance sheet so that you are aware of, and can manage, your company's risk, efficiency, and return on assets.

Ron Robichaud is managing director of Robichaud Financial Services, consultants to the home building industry specializing in merger and acquisition representation, exit strategy development, and financial services. Robichaud Financial Services is dedicated to helping maximize company value, execute strategies, increase profitability, grow companies strategically, and streamline operations. Read more about Robichaud Financial at www.robichaudfinancial.com.

12

Budgeting: The Basis for Profitable Endings

By Alan Hanbury, Jr., CGR, CAPS

The adage "failing to plan is planning to fail" is truer than many builders want to believe. The keys to a successful business year are to make an intelligent guess about what the end of the year will look like and set goals to reach the desired end. Therefore, builders should begin with the end in mind.

All goals and desires will have financial impact so they should be **SMART**:

- **S**pecific
- **M**easurable
- **A**ction oriented
- **R**ealistic
- **T**ime sensitive

A goal that can't be reviewed in these terms is merely a wish. For example, inflation can increase revenues. However, if increasing sales is the goal, a plan to increase residential sales revenues by 5% compounded over the next 3 years by increasing options, raising prices, and not adding staff is more realistic. It has a time frame and is specific, action-oriented, measurable, and with proper planning, realistic and attainable.

Clearly defined goals can help builders establish more accurate budgets. Think of your budget as an opportunity to anticipate your best year ever, while having a plan for making adjustments if the financial picture sours. With a sound budget, if the year is going better than planned, or even stellar, you will have already chosen the programs, purchases, marketing, hiring, salary, and other pieces of your business plan. If the year is going poorly, you will have a written list of the nonessential programs and expenses, possible layoffs, and you will know which capital purchases will not be made. With a predictable budget cycle, you have made the hard decisions on paper outside of the emotionally charged climate that exists at the time of the actual cutbacks.

To judge whether you are having a good year, a year better than last, or your best year ever, measure both volume and gross profit margin. These two measurements can predict accurately the year-end outcome of your labors.

With the IRS allowing for first year Section 179 depreciation write-offs of up to $125,000, it is easy to play the tax and profit game on capital purchases right up until you actually have to pay your taxes, but other tax issues and timing might need to play out before the year's end. Selling for a loss or gain; contributing more—or conversely, nothing—to a pension plan; postponing invoice mailings; or collecting checks can help builders achieve their goals for the year.

The following five steps will help builders and remodelers create a budget that predicts a pricing model, forces decisions based on their impact on finances and production, and can be tracked monthly.

Step 1: Understand Overhead

Start with the results from the most recent year, using your tax form, off-the-shelf or industry-specific accounting package, or a computerized checkbook. Historical data is useful as well. Budget for items that will increase in cost by more than inflation. Liability insurance, workers' compensation, health insurance, and utilities might be among these expenses. Next, add expense items that you have some control over but want to increase. These might be a Web site, new job signs, marketing materials, additional employees, raises, increased benefits, or other items.

Finally, look at the balance of your chart of accounts and determine the best use for business revenues. Even a soft economy requires business investment. Education, for example, might include attending the International Builders' Show and other NAHB-sponsored symposia and meetings, joining a 20 Club, working toward your Certified Graduate Builder or Graduate Master Builder designation, or purchasing books from BuilderBooks.com. Registration costs, lodging, food, and time away from producing income all need to be factored into these investments.

When you are comfortable that your proposed budget reflects both your personal and business goals, decide whether or not to cover the expenses—either fully or partially—in the current year. Note the month in which you plan to start expensing items so only that portion of the annual cost is reflected in the current year's budget. The annualized expenses can help in planning the following year's budget.

Step 2: Budget With Profit in Mind

The industry standard for profit is usually as much as 10% of revenue. That is a reasonable target, but as your company matures you should be searching for ways to build assets that could be a retirement vehicle or income stream for the owner, rather than focusing on showing a net profit (which is immediately taxable). Still, strive for the equivalent of six months of overhead in retained earnings before letting up on the net profit goals. Find a target volume in net profit dollars rather than a net profit percentage; a fixed dollar amount is an easier number to work with. Step 4 will confirm whether the dollar amount is a legitimate or attainable goal.

One final note on Step 2: Aim high because gravity will pull your arrow lower than the bull's eye at which you were aiming. Never plan for a break-even year; they will come all too often without planning for one. If you have balloon payments or capital purchases looming, if the long-term trend for your specialty is falling, or if you are posturing for sale, bonding, or a loan package, keep net profit a business priority.

Step 3: Determine Owner's Compensation

For remodeling, the industry standard for owner's compensation is 10% of sales, including benefits, for companies with revenues up to $2.5 to $3 million. A builder's starting goal should be at least 7% but no less than 3%. An alternative benchmark is a minimum of $60,000 for each owner or 20% more than your highest paid employee (measured in annual compensation for salaried employees, or 20% above the highest hourly rate). Using an hourly rate, multiply the sum by the number of hours you work, which probably will end up being 20% more than your full-time employees. In years with sufficient retained earnings, boost the salary multiplier and reduce your net profit. In any case, you should have as much as 15% of revenues (10% + 5%) available to choose between pay for yourself and net profit for the business entity. These alternatives are available whether you are a sole proprietor, LLC, S Corp, or C Corp.

Step 4: Make Sales Predictions Based on Actual Revenue

Start with the previous year's revenue, rather than sales. Production is the linchpin of home building and remodeling, and the most helpful gauge of future profits. Assess sales per employee as well. My company tracks revenue per salesperson, or per full-time-equivalent employee, because we do not employ full-timers. Therefore, we track by revenue per hour of sale efforts. Examining production per field employee reveals whether the company needs to hire additional people to achieve the revenue goals. If your company uses project managers or construction superintendents, track revenue per project manager as well.

The amount of sales per management employee reveals whether office support staffing is sufficient to keep up with the administrative functions. If paperwork is not timely and if reports are not generated for decision-making, businesses are flying blind, perhaps even making decisions based on a checkbook balance.

Watch the trends. NAHB chief economist Dave Seiders regularly reports on materials costs and availability, demand for services and products (including both single-family and multifamily construction and remodeling), the cost of money, inflation, and other trends that impact the business of building. Housing Economics Online, an online subscription newsletter, provides the latest in-depth economic analysis from NAHB's Economics Group.

Finally, remember that more companies die from indigestion than starvation—periods of growth can be deadlier than market slowdowns. Growth without attention to cash-flow management or access to funding is the proverbial kiss of death. Aim for growth of not more than 10 times working capital (current assets − current liabilities) or no more than 12 times your working capital ratio (working capital ÷ sales).

Project growth wisely. A company with $100,000 of current assets and $123,000 in current liabilities should not plan to grow at all, since it is, at least in the short term, bankrupt. Reversing the numbers, the working capital would be $23,000. If sales are $1 million, working capital would be 2.3% ($23,000 ÷ $1,000,000). Given these numbers, the maximum safe growth for this company would be $230,000 (10 × $23,000).

Learn from the past. Enter your revenues and expenses into a spreadsheet and track them by month. With a four-column format you can include one for last year's historical results, one for the coming year's budget, one for each month's actual expenses, and one for variance from the budget (in dollars or percentages). A fifth column may be added to track both dollars and percentages so you can see whether the difference is material or marginal.

Make sure your plan works. What margin and markup are required to make this plan work? To find out, combine overhead with owner's compensation, adding a profit goal in dollars. Then divide the total into the projected sales volume. For example, if owner's compensation is $100,000, profit is $100,000, and overhead is $160,000, gross profit must equal $360,000. If the sales prediction is $1.2 million, then the gross margin needed is $360,000 ÷ $120,000 or 30%.

To determine markup, use the following equation:

$$\text{margin} \div (1 - \text{margin}).$$

For example, $0.30 \div (1 - .30) = 42.86\%$.

The following equation produces a markup multiplier:

$$1 \div (1 - \text{margin})$$

For the above margin of 0.30, the equation is $1 \div 0.7 = 1.4286$.

Beginning with a target percentage of profit to determine markup, add overhead and owner's compensation to determine a break-even gross profit margin, and then add 10%. Divide overhead and owner's compensation by the sales prediction to find the breakeven. Again, using the previous example, the equation would be $260,000 ÷ $1,200,000 = 21.666%. Add 10% (your target margin) and the result is 31.666 gross margin. Using the equation for markup, the calculation looks like this: $0.3167 \div 0.6833 = 46.35$. The markup multiplier would be 1.4635.

Wait . . . account for slippage! Any budget can be assembled and a pricing model calculated before the first nail is driven. However, each company has a silent partner—slippage. The average in the home building industry is almost 5%, so this partner routinely takes home $50,000 of every $1 million in volume. Add this difference between theoretical margin and produced margin and redo your markup calculations. Whereas slippage can result from many things, the primary cause is poor estimating skills caused by lack of, or poorly performed, job costing. Therefore, even as you account for slippage in your numbers, you must root out its cause.

Benchmarking, writing down your targets, communicating with staff to get them on board with your profit goals, controlling overhead, rooting out the causes of slippage, and increasing employee efficiency are the keys to success and safe growth.

Step 5: Don't Underestimate the Cost of Labor

The actual cost of any hour of labor is often 60% more than the nominal hourly rate and in some cases almost 100% greater, so a business will never make gross profit targets if it is not accounting accurately for labor costs. Federal Insurance Contributions Act (FICA), Federal Unemployment Tax Act (FUTA), State Unemployment Tax Act (SUTA), workers' compensation, general liability insurance, health insurance, vacation, holiday, personal time, sick time, training and education, tool and gas allowances, and picnics, parties and gifts, are additional labor costs. They should be accounted for in direct costs, not overhead, to predict pricing.

After determining total costs, examine billable hours, rather than paid hours. When pricing jobs, budget all employment costs as direct costs, regardless of the week they are incurred, by using a labor burden multiplier for every hour charged to jobs. QuickBooks and all industry-specific accounting packages allow for this, so use them.

Find your break-even point. Breakeven is the point at which overhead and gross profit (and no net profit) are covered. To calculate breakeven, divide your gross profit margin (actual, after slippage; not theoretical) into your overhead before profit. In the previous example, if actual gross profit was 33.33 and you anticipate $260,000 of overhead, breakeven would be $780,000 or ($260,000 ÷ 0.333). All revenue over $780,000 provides a 33% gross profit margin and 33% net profit!

By understanding markup and slippage, builders and remodelers can calculate the revenue needed for the year. Divide overhead and profit by the theoretical margin created by your markup, minus your slippage percentage. With 50% markup, the equation would be as follows:

$$0.5 \div (1 + 0.5) \text{ or } 0.5 \div 1.5 = 0.3333$$

Adding 4.67% for historical slippage, the result is 38%, which translates to a 61% markup. In other words, you need to add 11% markup to cover 5% of slippage!

If overhead increases at the same percentage or more with increased volume, less profit will result. Additional volume increases challenges for the office, field, sales staff, and the owner, whose judgment may be compromised by running too far and too fast. Be forewarned: There is only one Wal-Mart. If a business is not making money at its current sales volume, the company is unlikely to pull everything together with even more sales. Instead, it will merely go out of business faster!

The following cost-benefit analysis method can help you determine whether additional volume will generate enough profit to cover expenses such as another truck, additional staff, hardware and software, or other investments to maintain or grow your business.

Divide the expected cost by the margin produced (after slippage) to find the additional volume needed at that margin to cover the added expense. If existing overhead will increase as well, add that to the cost of the proposed new item and recalculate the math. New items might include a cell phone, desk, calculator, license for another CAD seat, or auto allowance, in addition to labor burden. A salesperson at $50,000 could really be an investment of $85,000, when benefits and ancillary costs are taken into account. You would need $255,000 of additional volume at 33.33% gross margin, $340,000 of additional volume to break even with a 25% margin, and $425,000 more in volume with a 20% margin. Pay particular attention to this if you are growing, because most of your growth will fuel expenses and not net profit!

Builders who can account for all of their costs, pass most through to clients in direct costs, control overhead, reach or exceed target revenues, and sell at the needed markups will be successful.

Alan Hanbury is a popular speaker, a columnist for Remodeling *magazine, and previously a columnist for* Professional Remodeler *magazine. He is also an instructor for the NAHB University of Housing designation programs and sits on NAHB's Education and Business Management and Information Technology committees. He can be reached at 860-666-1537 or e-mail alanh@houseofhanbury.com.*

Financial Ratios: Valuable Management Tools for All Home Builders

By Raymond D. Nan and Mary Alice Hewitt

Financial ratios are not just for Wall Street. They are important tools that every business owner needs to be able to use. By understanding these indicators of business performance, companies can control costs, use capital more efficiently, and reap bigger profits.

Ratios allow a company to identify its financial and operational strengths and weaknesses, helping pinpoint where to focus efforts in the future to achieve greater success. They reveal how a company performs, operationally and financially, relative to industry standards. Analyzing and comparing ratios to industry standards may signal corrective actions to improve future performance and/or reduce business risk.

Moreover, knowing and understanding your ratios will allow you to make the best use of *The Cost of Doing Business Study*.

Despite these benefits, many small-volume builders may not understand the importance of financial ratios. The word *ratio* in finance does not refer to the basic mathematical principle with which many of us are familiar. For example, if you've watched any team sporting event, you probably know what it means when a team's stats of, say 15-5-2 appear. This list of numbers, or ratio, means that the team has 15 wins, 5 losses, and 2 ties. Financial ratios, however, are quite different. They restate accounting data, from prior periods and in relative terms, to identify some of the financial and operational strengths and weaknesses of a company. These ratios draw on specific pieces of financial information to arrive at numerical values that indicate performance for various categories.

Table 13.1 Basic financial ratios

Categories	Formulas
Liquidity ratios	
Current ratio	current assets/current liabilities
Cash ratio	(cash + marketable securities)/current liabilities
Net working capital	current assets − current liabilities
Asset turnover ratios	
Total asset turnover	sales/total assets
Leverage ratios	
Total debt ratio	total liabilities/total assets
Short-term debt ratio	current liabilities/current assets
Total debt-to-equity ratio	total liabilities/equity
Cost ratios	
Gross margin %	(sales − all direct costs)/sales
Cost of sales %	all direct costs/sales
Operating expense %	all indirect costs/sales
Interest expense %	total interest expense/sales
AP-days payable turnover	cost of sales/accounts receivable turnover
Profitability ratios	
Profit margin	earnings before taxes/sales
Return on assets	earnings before taxes/total assets
Return on equity	earnings before taxes/equity

Limitations of Financial Ratios

Despite the benefits of analyzing performance using financial ratios, it is important to remember that the process is not foolproof. Keep the following caveats in mind before making drastic changes based on financial ratio analysis:[4]

- Ratios are general indicators that may not necessarily tell the whole story. Since ratio values are based on calculations using company accounting information, and because accounting data are often subject to estimation, a company's ratios may not represent a precise measurement of a company's performance at a given point in time. Rather, ratios should only be viewed as approximate indicators of performance.
- One ratio may contradict others, so consider calculating and analyzing a wide range of ratios.
- Look behind and beyond ratios for the factors that may be driving a company's numbers. Ratios alone should not be the totality of your

---

[4] Gleim, Irvin and Flesher, Dale. *CFM Review: Part 2, 11th edition*. Florida: Gleim Publications, 2002.

business analysis and improvement efforts. When ratios seem to conflict, don't simply assume that the numbers are wrong, but don't take favorable numbers at face value either. Rather, think about the various facets of your operations and financing that may be causing your numbers to look favorable or unfavorable.

■ Certain standards may not apply to your business. What's good for one company may not be good for yours, so think about the context of your company's results before taking action. For example, you may want to be financially aggressive, meaning that you don't want to hold a lot of excess cash, but would rather invest it in new equipment, land, or short-term financial investments. In this case, the liquidity standards of the industry may be less relevant for your business. The risk preference of the company (or builder) should drive operating, investment, and financing decisions.

■ Not every company uses the same fiscal year. When comparing your financial results to industry standards, make sure you are using the same fiscal periods. Otherwise, your comparisons may be questionable.

Financial Ratios as a Group

Collectively, financial ratios help to explain the overall financial and operational performance of your company. However, when viewed individually, each ratio measures a specific aspect of performance. For example, current ratio measures a company's ability to pay its short-term obligations and liabilities. Conversely, debt ratio indicates what proportion of debt a company has relative to its assets.

Financial ratios may be subdivided into the following categories:

■ liquidity
■ asset turnover
■ leverage
■ cost
■ profitability

Liquidity Ratios

Liquidity ratios measure the ability of a firm to pay its short-term financial obligations. These ratios indicate how much cash, cash equivalents, accounts receivable, and inventory a firm has to pay off its short-term obligations, and how quickly a firm can convert its liquid assets (accounts receivable and inventories) into cash. One ratio in this category is the current ratio. Inventory, accounts receivable, cash, and marketable securities are considered current assets when calculating the current ratio. The formula is as follows:

$$\text{current ratio} = \frac{\text{current assets}}{\text{current liabilities}}$$

Since the current ratio is a measure of a company's ability to pay its short-term obligations with all of its current assets, the ratio should be greater than 1, meaning a company has positive working capital.

The cash ratio is similar to the current ratio, with a key difference—the cash ratio calculation does not include inventory or accounts receivable. As a result, it is a more stringent test of liquidity than the current ratio. The equation should also be greater than 1, as a negative value means that a company would be unable to pay off all of its short-term obligations if they became due immediately. The equation is:

$$\text{cash ratio} = \frac{\text{cash} + \text{marketable securities}}{\text{current liabilities}}$$

Net working capital (NWC) specifies the liquid financial resources a firm has available after all short-term obligations have been paid. It is a measure of a company's short-term financial health. The equation is as follows:

$$\text{NWC} = \text{current assets} - \text{current liabilities}$$

A positive working capital value means that a company has more than enough current assets to pay off its short-term liabilities, even if internal and/or external factors of the business become unfavorable. A negative value means a company may have trouble meeting its short-term liability requirements with current assets under the same unexpectedly unfavorable situation.

Asset Turnover Ratios

As a group, asset turnover ratios help answer, "Is a company generating adequate operating profits on its assets?" Although this category includes a number of ratios, measuring a firm's use of assets to produce income and revenue, the most commonly applied one in the construction industry is the total asset turnover ratio. The asset turnover ratio indicates management's effectiveness at managing a firm's balance sheet (e.g., assets) as indicated by the amount of sales generated per one dollar of assets.

$$\text{total asset turnover} = \frac{\text{sales}}{\text{total assets}}$$

Leverage Ratios

Leverage ratios describe how a firm is financed. More specifically, these ratios measure the extent to which debt is used in financing operations. The total debt ratio indicates the proportion of debt a company has relative to its assets.[5] Its value should be less than one, meaning that a company has more assets than debt. The equation for determining this ratio is as follows:

$$\text{total debt ratio} = \frac{\text{total liabilities}}{\text{total assets}}$$

Total liabilities include both short- (one year or less) and long-term (more than a year) construction loans, any other long-term debt, and short-term notes payable.

The short-term debt ratio is the percentage of current assets that are offset by current liabilities:

$$\text{short-term debt ratio} = \frac{\text{current liabilities}}{\text{current assets}}$$

Finally, total debt-to-equity indicates how much debt a company uses to finance its assets relative to owner's equity. This ratio indicates whether a business is conservatively financed (with little debt) or aggressively financed (with high debt). A high total debt-to-equity ratio indicates that a company is aggressively financing its growth with debt. The equation is as follows:

$$\text{total debt-to-equity} = \frac{\text{total liabilities}}{\text{equity}}$$

[5] Keown, Arthur et. al. *Financial Management: Principles and Applications, 10th edition.* New Jersey: Prentice Hall, 2004.

Cost Ratios

As the name implies, cost ratios measure the ability of a firm to control costs. One of the most important ratios to determine and examine when doing financial ratio analysis is the gross margin percentage. The gross margin percentage is the percentage of $1 of sales that is left over after subtracting these direct costs to make a product. In other words, it is the percentage of each dollar of revenue that is retained by a company and put toward other business operations, such as operating expenses.

The equation for determining gross margin percentage is as follows:

$$\text{gross margin \%} = \frac{(\text{sales} - \text{all direct costs})}{\text{sales}}$$

The cost of sales percentage (or cost of goods sold percentage) indicates a firm's ability to control its direct costs, relative to sales. The smaller the ratio's value, the more efficient and effective a firm is at controlling its direct costs relative to sales.

$$\text{cost of sales \%} = \frac{\text{all direct costs}}{\text{sales}}$$

Operating expenses are the essential indirect expenditures a company must make to stay in business. The operating expense percentage includes sales and marketing, finance, general and administration, and miscellaneous overhead at a project (e.g., fixed costs, such as depreciation on field equipment and office equipment). The formula is as follows:

$$\text{operating expense percentage} = \frac{\text{all indirect costs}}{\text{sales}}$$

Another important cost management ratio is the interest expense percentage. With this equation, total interest expense includes the cost of borrowing money for both short- and long-term loans:

$$\text{interest expense percentage} = \frac{\text{total interest expense}}{\text{sales}}$$

Lastly, the accounts payable/days payable turnover ratio equals the average time, in days, that a bill remains unpaid by a firm. In order to take advantage of supplier discounts, as well as to maintain good communication and relations with his or her suppliers and vendors, a builder may consider an optimal range, such as 10 days (for 2/10, net 30 supplier discounts) to 30 days (for firms that have only contractual agreements, with payment schedules) for payments to vendors. The equation is as follows:

$$\text{AP days payable} = \frac{\text{cost of goods sold}}{\text{accounts receivable turnover}^6}$$

The AP days payable turnover ratio is an important indicator of whether a builder is taking advantage of its supplier discounts. If not, then the builder is paying more for those goods or services than he or she needs to. The overage could amount to thousands or even tens of thousands of dollars per year!

Profitability Ratios

Profitability ratios are the final category of financial ratios. These ratios measure the earnings of a firm in relation to a base figure, usually sales. Within this category of ratios, profit margin is a key statistic every business owner should be aware of. The profit margin measures how much out of every dollar of sales a company keeps in earnings, after subtracting direct costs (cost of goods sold, including direct materials, direct labor, direct overhead in the field, and land costs) and indirect costs (operating expenses, including general and administrative expenses, financing expenses, and marketing expenses) from sales. For example, if a company has a 15% profit margin, then that company has a net income of $0.15 (before taxes) for each dollar of sales. Profit margin values also are useful to compare the performance of different firms. Those with high profit margins may have more sales relative to other firms, or may have implemented total quality management (TQM) in their processes to reduce costs, minimize wasteful spending, and provide more operational efficiency and effectiveness. The equation for determining profit margin is as follows:

$$\text{profit margin} = \frac{\text{earnings before taxes}}{\text{sales}}$$

---

[6] $\text{accounts receivable turnover} = \dfrac{\text{annual sales}}{\text{average accounts receivable}}$

Return on assets indicates how efficient management is at using assets to generate earnings. When shown as a percentage, this value is also known as return on investment. The formula is as follows:

$$\text{return on assets} = \frac{\text{earnings before taxes}}{\text{total assets}}$$

Last, but certainly not least, is the return-on-equity ratio. Return on equity reveals how much profit a company generates with the money it is investing in the company (ownership in the company). Overall, this ratio is an indicator of how well a company is investing its money. If the value is low, the money could be put to better use. It is calculated as follows:

$$\text{return-on-equity} = \frac{\text{earnings before taxes}}{\text{equity}}$$

While calculating these ratios is only half the battle when it comes to financial analysis and business improvement, they are a valuable lens through which to view your company's performance—and to compare it with the performance of the home building industry as a whole. All builders, regardless of size, should incorporate financial ratios into a thorough analysis of their company's financial health and business processes. Doing this regularly over time will enable you to see how far your business has come, and will empower you to make good decisions that will help you grow and improve in the future.

Raymond D. Nan is an accountant and financial analyst at EYA LLC, an urban residential developer in the greater Washington, D.C., area.

Mary Alice Hewitt is an NAHB staff member.

Glossary

balance sheet. A statement that shows the wealth of a company at a given time by identifying the types and amounts of assets owned as well as the types of liabilities incurred

builder with land costs. Single-family home builder whose firm builds and sells homes on land it develops or purchases (already developed)

builder without land costs (custom builder). Single-family home builder whose firm builds exclusively on land owned by its customers

combination builder. Single-family home builder whose firm builds both on land it develops/purchases and on land owned by its customers

cost of goods sold. Sum of land costs, single-family home building direct construction costs (e.g., permits, materials, labor), residential remodeling direct construction costs, light commercial and multifamily direct construction costs, and indirect construction costs (non-unit specific costs such as job supervision and warranty costs).

current ratio. A measure of *balance sheet* liquidity. It equals current assets divided by current liabilities.

debt-to-equity ratio. Total liabilities divided by *owner's equity*

gross profit. Total revenue minus the *cost of goods sold*

gross profit margin. Gross profit divided by total revenue

income statement. Among a company's most valuable financial statements, the income statement identifies specific revenue and expense types and their amounts, revealing whether the business earned a profit during a specified period. The basic structure of an income statement is as follows:

$$\text{revenue} - \text{cost of goods sold} = \text{gross profit}$$
$$\text{gross profit} - \text{operating expenses} = \text{net profit}$$

net profit. Gross profit minus operating expenses

net profit margin. Net profit divided by total revenue

operating expenses. Sum of financing expenses, sales and marketing expenses, general and administrative expenses, and owner's compensation.

owner's equity. Difference between assets and liabilities; a company's wealth. Owner's equity is calculated as follows:

$$\text{assets} - \text{liabilities} = \text{owner's equity}$$

production builder. Single-family home builder with 26 or more closings in 2006

small-volume builder. Single-family home builder with 25 or fewer closings in 2006

Appendix **I**

Detailed Tables

Table 1 Indicate your firm's main operation during fiscal 2006 (% of respondents)

	Total	Region				Total revenue ($ in millions)				Number of homes closed				Type of builder		
		North-east	Mid-west	South	West	<2	2–4.9	5–9.9	≥10	<10	10–25	26–99	≥100	With land costs	Without land costs	Combo builder
Single-family production builder	36	23	30	41	45	15	18	27	71	12	33	74	82	66	11	23
Single-family custom builder (on owner's lot)	26	33	27	23	30	40	34	43	8	50	27	3		5	67	40
Single-family custom builder (on builder's lot)	24	18	25	25	19	22	29	23	14	26	33	19	11	22	11	33
Multifamily builder (condo/co-op units)	2	8	4		2		4	3	3	1	4	3		1	4	1
Multifamily builder (for-rent units)	1	3		2			2		1	1				2		
Land developer	1	5		1		3			1	2	1		4	1		1
Residential remodeling/ rehabilitation	8	10	13	7		18	13	3	2	7	2			3	7	
Other	2	3	1	1	4	1	2		2	1	2		4	1		1

Table 2 Indicate all other operations (% of respondents)

	Total	Region				Total revenue ($ in millions)				Number of homes closed				Type of builder		
		North-east	Mid-west	South	West	<2	2–4.9	5–9.9	≥10	<10	10–25	26–99	≥100	With land costs	Without land costs	Combo builder
Single-family production builder	7	10	3	11	4	12	6	0	7	8	8	11	0	9	7	7
Single-family custom builder (on owner's lot)	29	27	34	29	25	16	33	22	31	23	41	31	29	13	17	48
Single-family custom builder (on builder's lot)	35	37	40	35	29	42	44	35	34	42	38	31	24	27	28	51
Multifamily builder—condo/co-op units	12	10	14	13	7	2	3	4	23	5	3	14	33	15	0	10
Multifamily builder—for-rent units	6	7	10	1	7	5	6	0	5	4	3	8	5	7	0	4
Land developer	34	23	29	37	36	9	28	35	55	13	31	64	57	45	3	35
Residential remodeling/rehabilitation	35	53	41	27	25	42	42	48	16	51	41	14	5	16	66	39
Other	13	20	16	9	11	14	17	13	11	15	15	8	5	13	14	8

Table 3 Percent of your business from each operation (average % share)

	Total	Region				Total revenue ($ in millions)				Number of homes closed				Type of builder		
		North-east	Mid-west	South	West	<2	2–4.9	5–9.9	≥10	<10	10–25	26–99	≥100	With land costs	Without land costs	Combo builder
Single-family production builder	29.8	20.4	23.8	32.8	40.4	11.4	13.8	21.9	61.5	9.3	25.1	61.3	78.3	58.9	4.7	16.0
Single-family custom builder (on owner's lot)	24.0	27.8	24.0	20.3	32.3	32.7	30.3	37.6	8.5	40.7	29.7	4.9	0.9	4.7	63.4	31.7
Single-family custom builder (on builder's lot)	22.9	19.7	23.5	26.2	15.0	24.6	31.5	24.7	14.2	27.5	30.9	20.2	7.7	21.1	14.0	34.3
Multifamily builder (condo/co-op units)	4.1	6.4	4.8	3.1	3.3	0.8	3.0	4.0	6.2	2.1	3.3	7.0	3.9	3.6	2.7	4.0
Multifamily builder (for-rent units)	0.9	0.5	1.2	0.9	0.2	0.3	2.4	0.0	0.3	1.3	0.2	0.6	0.0	1.4	0.0	0.4
Land developer	4.0	6.4	2.4	4.4	3.9	3.3	2.2	3.0	5.5	2.9	2.8	5.5	6.1	4.7	0.2	5.2
Residential remodeling/ rehabilitation	10.8	12.8	16.6	9.9	1.0	21.9	13.7	8.0	0.4	13.0	3.6	0.2	0.0	3.8	13.5	4.4
Other	3.5	6.1	3.7	2.5	4.0	5.1	3.1	0.8	3.4	3.1	4.3	0.4	3.2	1.8	1.5	4.1

Table 4 Status of firm's operating head (% of respondents)

	Total	Region				Total revenue ($ in millions)				Number of homes closed				Type of builder		
		North-east	Mid-west	South	West	<2	2–4.9	5–9.9	≥10	<10	10–25	26–99	≥100	With land costs	Without land costs	Combo builder
Principal owner	73	85	72	69	76	71	73	86	69	79	74	72	58	69	81	79
Sole owner	19	15	18	22	17	25	24	14	14	20	21	16	19	21	19	13
Salaried executive only (not a principal owner)	6		8	7	5	2	2		12	1	2	11	15	9		4
Other	2		1	3	2	2			5		2	2	8	1		4

Table 5 Years firm has been in residential construction business (% of respondents)

	Total	Region				Total revenue ($ in millions)				Number of homes closed				Type of builder		
		North-east	Mid-west	South	West	<2	2–4.9	5–9.9	≥10	<10	10–25	26–99	≥100	With land costs	Without land costs	Combo builder
≤10	21		18	32	15	26	26	13	14	24	22	14	20	25	13	18
11–19	29	35	30	21	38	26	30	42	30	32	31	25	24	27	29	32
20+	51	65	52	47	46	47	45	46	55	43	47	61	56	48	58	50
Average	21	27	23	19	19	20	19	20	23	19	20	24	23	21	23	21
Median	20	23.5	20	17	15	17	16	18.5	20	17	17	21.5	22	18	21	19.5

Table 6 Income statement (average in $1,000s)

	Total	Region				Total revenue ($ in millions)				Number of homes closed				Type of builder		
		North-east	Mid-west	South	West	<2	2–4.9	5–9.9	≥10	<10	10–25	26–99	≥100	With land costs	Without land costs	Combo builder
Revenue																
Single-family home building	16,381	10,966	13,232	18,579	20,214	1,024	2,941	6,774	37,479	2,276	6,077	18,404	80,558	25,208	3,636	11,871
Residential remodeling	138	206	218	106	49	98	227	308	56	227	114	31	74	47	322	140
Multifamily	1,393	1,186	2,571	1,348	16	2	107	36	3,502	15	308	705	6,419	1,305	796	711
Light commercial/industrial	127	365	88	120	24	26	81	78	237	59	422	52	42	62	24	306
All other revenue	647	431	464	746	884	22	152	130	1,515	64	265	1,095	2,759	943	89	703
Total revenue	18,686	13,153	16,572	20,899	21,187	1,172	3,508	7,325	42,790	2,640	7,186	20,287	89,852	27,564	4,865	13,731
Costs of goods sold																
Land costs	2,929	1,548	2,777	3,203	3,603	86	352	700	7,035	226	609	3,469	15,032	4,671	0	2,076
Single-family home building direct construction costs	9,809	6,159	8,514	10,786	12,308	721	2,131	4,652	21,960	1,659	4,317	10,716	46,679	14,342	2,958	7,725
Residential remodeling direct construction costs	90	135	158	55	38	67	147	182	41	135	80	23	47	27	196	80
Multifamily direct construction costs	866	951	1,564	788	9	0	69	29	2,176	0	294	508	3,856	765	671	464
Light commercial/industrial direct construction costs	98	292	68	96	0	17	58	59	187	39	344	48	0	45	14	242
Indirect construction costs	605	421	513	760	544	56	111	227	1,379	102	261	771	2,503	856	233	438
All other costs of goods sold	402	619	256	417	429	10	25	79	985	19	101	471	2,518	774	20	247
Total cost of goods sold	14,799	10,126	13,850	16,104	16,931	957	2,894	5,927	33,762	2,179	6,007	16,005	70,635	21,481	4,092	11,272

(continued)

Table 6 Continued

	Total	Region				Total revenue ($ in millions)				Number of homes closed				Type of builder		
		North-east	Mid-west	South	West	<2	2–4.9	5–9.9	≥10	<10	10–25	26–99	≥100	With land costs	Without land costs	Combo builder
Gross profit	**3,887**	**3,027**	**2,721**	**4,795**	**4,256**	**214**	**614**	**1,398**	**9,029**	**461**	**1,180**	**4,282**	**19,217**	**6,083**	**773**	**2,459**
Median gross profit	966	971	725	1,094	1,247	190	569	1,231	4,838	336	730	3,388	14,910	2,474	476	729
Operating expenses																
Financing expense	462	163	602	479	467	20	61	167	1,084	45	127	554	2,286	737	24	327
Sales and marketing expense	827	399	570	1,160	795	21	92	206	1,991	53	228	1,036	3,784	1,241	74	573
General and administrative expense	927	613	757	1,093	1,060	92	178	462	2,066	157	413	938	4,328	1,299	325	694
Owner's compensation	239	318	136	235	333	67	121	202	434	96	193	335	604	311	136	203
Total operating expenses	2,456	1,494	2,065	2,968	2,655	200	452	1,037	5,575	351	962	2,862	11,002	3,587	559	1,798
Net income before taxes	**1,431**	**1,533**	**656**	**1,827**	**1,601**	**14**	**162**	**361**	**3,454**	**110**	**218**	**1,420**	**8,215**	**2,496**	**214**	**661**
Median net income before taxes	193	266	116	253	305	23	121	334	1,350	70	149	974	6,475	611	65	149

Table 7 Income statement (% share of revenue)

	Total	Region				Total revenue ($ in millions)				Number of homes closed				Type of builder		
		North-east	Mid-west	South	West	<2	2–4.9	5–9.9	≥10	<10	10–25	26–99	≥100	With land costs	Without land costs	Combo builder
Revenue																
Single-family home building	87.7	83.4	79.8	88.9	95.4	87.4	83.8	92.5	87.6	86.2	84.6	90.7	89.7	91.5	74.7	86.5
Residential remodeling	0.7	1.6	1.3	0.5	0.2	8.4	6.5	4.2	0.1	8.6	1.6	0.2	0.1	0.2	6.6	1.0
Multifamily	7.5	9.0	15.5	6.5	0.1	0.2	3.1	0.5	8.2	0.6	4.3	3.5	7.1	4.7	16.4	5.2
Light commercial/industrial	0.7	2.8	0.5	0.6	0.1	2.2	2.3	1.1	0.6	2.2	5.9	0.3	0.0	0.2	0.5	2.2
All other revenue	3.5	3.3	2.8	3.6	4.2	1.9	4.3	1.8	3.5	2.4	3.7	5.4	3.1	3.4	1.8	5.1
Total revenue	100.0	100.0	100.0	100.0	100.0	100.0	100.0	100.0	100.0	100.0	100.0	100.0	100.0	100.0	100.0	100.0
Costs of goods sold																
Land costs	15.7	11.8	16.8	15.3	17.0	7.3	10.0	9.6	16.4	8.6	8.5	17.1	16.7	16.9	0.0	15.1
Single-family home building direct construction costs	52.5	46.8	51.4	51.6	58.1	61.5	60.7	63.5	51.3	62.8	60.1	52.8	52.0	52.0	60.8	56.3
Residential remodeling direct construction costs	0.5	1.0	1.0	0.3	0.2	5.7	4.2	2.5	0.1	5.1	1.1	0.1	0.1	0.1	4.0	0.6
Multifamily direct construction costs	4.6	7.2	9.4	3.8	0.0	0.0	2.0	0.4	5.1	0.0	4.1	2.5	4.3	2.8	13.8	3.4
Light commercial/industrial direct construction costs	0.5	2.2	0.4	0.5	0.0	1.5	1.7	0.8	0.4	1.5	4.8	0.2	0.0	0.2	0.3	1.8
Indirect construction costs	3.2	3.2	3.1	3.6	2.6	4.8	3.2	3.1	3.2	3.9	3.6	3.8	2.8	3.1	4.8	3.2
All other costs of goods sold	2.2	4.7	1.5	2.0	2.0	0.9	0.7	1.1	2.3	0.7	1.4	2.3	2.8	2.8	0.4	1.8
Total cost of goods sold	79.2	77.0	83.6	77.1	79.9	81.7	82.5	80.9	78.9	82.5	83.6	78.9	78.6	77.9	84.1	82.1

(continued)

Table 7 Continued

	Total	Region				Total revenue ($ in millions)				Number of homes closed				Type of builder		
		North-east	Mid-west	South	West	<2	2–4.9	5–9.9	≥10	<10	10–25	26–99	≥100	With land costs	Without land costs	Combo builder
Gross profit	20.8	23.0	16.4	22.9	20.1	18.3	17.5	19.1	21.1	17.5	16.4	21.1	21.4	22.1	15.9	17.9
Operating expenses																
Financing expense	2.5	1.2	3.6	2.3	2.2	1.7	1.7	2.3	2.5	1.7	1.8	2.7	2.5	2.7	0.5	2.4
Sales and marketing expense	4.4	3.0	3.4	5.6	3.8	1.8	2.6	2.8	4.7	2.0	3.2	5.1	4.2	4.5	1.5	4.2
General and administrative expense	5.0	4.7	4.6	5.2	5.0	7.8	5.1	6.3	4.8	5.9	5.7	4.6	4.8	4.7	6.7	5.1
Owner's compensation	1.3	2.4	0.8	1.1	1.6	5.7	3.4	2.8	1.0	3.6	2.7	1.7	0.7	1.1	2.8	1.5
Total operating expenses	13.1	11.4	12.5	14.2	12.5	17.1	12.9	14.2	13.0	13.3	13.4	14.1	12.2	13.0	11.5	13.1
Net income before taxes	7.7	11.7	4.0	8.7	7.5	1.2	4.6	4.9	8.1	4.2	3.0	7.0	9.1	9.1	4.4	4.8

Table 8 Balance sheet (average in $1,000s)

	Total	Region				Total revenue ($ in millions)				Number of homes closed				Type of builder		
		North-east	Mid-west	South	West	<2	2–4.9	5–9.9	≥10	<10	10–25	26–99	≥100	With land costs	Without land costs	Combo builder
Assets																
Cash	823	1,223	227	758	1,477	42	110	541	1,817	141	581	784	3,347	1,286	387	354
Construction work in progress	9,635	4,943	9,264	9,688	13,647	736	1,364	3,564	22,137	1,462	2,487	9,651	50,513	14,790	1,030	7,694
Other current assets	1,120	1,219	1,432	655	1,727	174	309	585	2,374	240	536	1,271	4,985	1,430	241	1,270
Other assets	1,382	409	871	1,712	2,087	104	289	513	3,003	148	680	2,014	5,818	1,822	208	1,569
Total assets	12,959	7,794	11,794	12,813	18,938	1,056	2,073	5,203	29,331	1,992	4,285	13,720	64,663	19,327	1,865	10,888
Liabilities																
Current liabilities	1,792	1,900	2,237	1,486	1,778	283	490	1,446	4,002	434	1,371	1,886	5,691	1,773	680	2,058
Construction loans	6,318	1,915	4,437	6,997	10,789	463	935	2,304	14,364	1,045	1,498	7,666	30,791	9,417	216	5,883
Other liabilities	1,438	474	2,670	1,068	1,342	127	328	317	3,294	220	448	841	9,095	2,525	354	743
Owner's equity	3,411	3,505	2,451	3,263	5,028	183	319	1,136	7,671	293	968	3,327	19,087	5,613	615	2,203
Total liabilities + equity	12,959	7,794	11,794	12,813	18,938	1,056	2,073	5,203	29,331	1,992	4,285	13,720	64,663	19,327	1,865	10,888

Table 9 Of single-family units closed in 2006, indicate how many were presold, speculative, and/or built on others' (customers') land (average number of homes closed)

Assets	Total	Region				Total revenue ($ in millions)				Number of homes closed				Type of builder		
		North-east	Mid-west	South	West	<2	2–4.9	5–9.9	≥10	<10	10–25	26–99	≥100	With land costs	Without land costs	Combo builder
Presold (on builder's lot)	29	22	30	32	26	1	3	6	76	1	6	31	179	50	0	22
Speculative	18	4	10	25	24	1	3	6	42	2	5	6	10	0	12	6
Built on others' land—customers	4	7	4	5	2	2	4	3	6	4	15	56	292	80	12	42
Total	52	32	44	63	52	4	10	15	124	20	38	55	61	63	0	52
(% share of units closed)																
Presold (on builder's lot)	57	68	69	51	49	17	28	40	62	30	31	35	35	37	0	33
Speculative	35	11	23	40	46	32	30	38	34	50	32	10	4	0	100	15
Built on others' land—customers	9	21	8	8	4	52	41	22	4	20	37	55	61	63	0	52
Total	100	100	100	100	100	100	100	100	100	100	100	100	100	100	100	100

Table 10 Of single-family units closed in 2006, indicate how many were built on lots your firm developed, on lots your firm purchased, and on others' (customers') land (average number of homes closed)

		Region				Total revenue ($ in millions)				Number of homes closed				Type of builder		
	Total	North-east	Mid-west	South	West	<2	2–4.9	5–9.9	≥10	<10	10–25	26–99	≥100	With land costs	Without land costs	Combo builder
Built on land my firm developed	28	22	28	27	37	1	3	6	73	0	6	26	180	50	0	18
Built on developed lots my firm purchased	19	3	13	31	13	1	3	6	46	1	5	24	102	30	0	17
Built on others' land—customers' land	4	7	3	5	2	2	4	3	6	2	5	6	10	0	12	6
Total	52	32	44	63	52	4	10	15	124	4	15	56	292	80	12	42
									(% share of units closed)							
Built on land my firm developed	54	69	63	43	70	21	30	36	59	12	37	47	62	62	0	44
Built on developed lots my firm purchased	37	10	29	49	26	27	30	42	37	36	32	43	35	38	0	41
Built on others' land—customers' land	9	21	8	8	4	52	41	22	4	51	31	10	4	0	100	15
Total	100	100	100	100	100	100	100	100	100	100	100	100	100	100	100	100

Table 11 Of single-family units closed in 2006, indicate how many were stick-built, modular, panelized, precut, or other (average number of homes closed)

	Region					Total revenue ($ in millions)				Number of homes closed				Type of builder		
	Total	North-east	Mid-west	South	West	<2	2–4.9	5–9.9	≥10	<10	10–25	26–99	≥100	With land costs	Without land costs	Combo builder
Stick-built	49	30	41	58	52	4	9	15	118	3	14	51	282	76	10	40
Modular	0	0	0	0	0	0	0	0	0	0	0	0	0	0	0	0
Panelized	2	2	2	4	0	0	1	0	6	0	1	4	10	4	1	1
Precut	0	0	0	0	0	0	0	0	0	0	0	0	0	0	0	0
Other	0	0	0	1	0	0	0	0	0	0	0	1	0	0	0	1
Total	52	32	44	63	52	4	10	15	124	4	15	56	292	80	12	42
(% share of units closed)																
Stick-built	95	94	95	93	100	90	89	100	95	91	92	91	96	95	90	95
Modular	0	0	0	0	0	7	0	0	0	2	1	0	0	0	0	0
Panelized	5	6	5	6	0	3	9	0	5	2	6	7	4	5	9	2
Precut	0	0	0	0	0	0	0	0	0	0	0	0	0	0	0	0
Other	1	0	0	1	0	0	2	0	0	4	1	2	0	0	1	2
Total	100	100	100	100	100	100	100	100	100	100	100	100	100	100	100	100

All single-family builders
Top and bottom 25% by net income before taxes

Table 12 Income statement (average in $1,000s)

	All	Top 25%	Bottom 25%
Revenue			
Single-family home building	16,381	25,635	9,001
Residential remodeling	138	140	71
Multifamily	1,393	270	1,079
Light commercial/industrial	127	12	134
All other revenue	647	1,073	554
Total revenue	18,686	27,130	10,839
Costs of goods sold			
Land costs	2,929	4,498	1,593
Single-family home building direct construction costs	9,809	13,749	6,434
Residential remodeling direct construction costs	90	94	65
Multifamily direct construction costs	866	161	792
Light commercial/industrial direct construction costs	98	9	97
Indirect construction costs	605	898	275
All other costs of goods sold	402	687	263
Total cost of goods sold	14,799	20,096	9,519
Gross profit	**3,887**	**7,035**	**1,320**
Operating expenses			
Financing expense	462	584	271
Sales and marketing expense	827	1,260	320
General and administrative expense	927	1,176	598
Owner's compensation	239	310	236
Total operating expenses	2,456	3,330	1,426
Net income before taxes	**1,431**	**3,705**	**(106)**

Table 13 Income statement (% share of revenue)

	All	Top 25%	Bottom 25%
Revenue			
Single-family home building	87.7	94.5	83.0
Residential remodeling	0.7	0.5	0.7
Multifamily	7.5	1.0	10.0
Light commercial/industrial	0.7	0.0	1.2
All other revenue	3.5	4.0	5.1
Total revenue	100.0	100.0	100.0
Costs of goods sold			
Land costs	15.7	16.6	14.7
Single-family home building direct construction costs	52.5	50.7	59.4
Residential remodeling direct construction costs	0.5	0.3	0.6
Multifamily direct construction costs	4.6	0.6	7.3
Light commercial/industrial direct construction costs	0.5	0.0	0.9
Indirect construction costs	3.2	3.3	2.5
All other costs of goods sold	2.2	2.5	2.4
Total cost of goods sold	79.2	74.1	87.8
Gross profit	**20.8**	**25.9**	**12.2**
Operating expenses			
Financing expense	2.5	2.2	2.5
Sales and marketing expense	4.4	4.6	3.0
General and administrative expense	5.0	4.3	5.5
Owner's compensation	1.3	1.1	2.2
Total operating expenses	13.1	12.3	13.2
Net income before taxes	**7.7**	**13.7**	**−1.0**

Table 14 Balance sheet (average in $1,000s)

	All	Top 25%	Bottom 25%
Assets			
Cash	823	1,349	741
Construction work in progress	9,635	13,316	9,473
Other current assets	1,120	1,857	884
Other assets	1,382	1,515	1,851
Total assets	12,959	18,037	12,949
Liabilities			
Current liabilities	1,792	2,222	1,874
Construction loans	6,318	8,815	7,631
Other liabilities	1,438	1,089	848
Owner's equity	3,411	5,911	2,596
Total liabilities and owner's equity	12,959	18,037	12,949

Builders with land costs
Top and bottom 25% by net income before taxes

Table 15 Income statement (average in $1,000s)

	All	Top 25%	Bottom 25%
Revenue			
Single-family home building	25,208	37,898	13,465
Residential remodeling	47	0	41
Multifamily	1,305	459	0
Light commercial/industrial	62	6	111
All other revenue	943	1,136	917
Total revenue	27,564	39,500	14,534
Costs of goods sold			
Land costs	4,671	6,718	2,026
Single-family home building direct construction costs	14,342	19,365	9,572
Residential remodeling direct construction costs	27	0	16
Multifamily direct construction costs	765	233	0
Light commercial/industrial direct construction costs	45	5	64
Indirect construction costs	856	1,390	202
All other costs of goods sold	774	865	643
Total cost of goods sold	21,481	28,576	12,522
Gross profit	**6,083**	**10,924**	**2,012**
Operating expenses			
Financing expense	737	748	288
Sales and marketing expense	1,241	1,856	548
General and administrative expense	1,299	1,758	836
Owner's compensation	311	384	329
Total operating expenses	3,587	4,746	2,001
Net income before taxes	**2,496**	**6,178**	**11**

Table 16 Income statement (% share of revenue)

	All	Top 25%	Bottom 25%
Revenue			
Single-family home building	91.5	95.9	92.6
Residential remodeling	0.2	0.0	0.3
Multifamily	4.7	1.2	0.0
Light commercial/industrial	0.2	0.0	0.8
All other revenue	3.4	2.9	6.3
Total revenue	100.0	100.0	100.0
Costs of goods sold			
Land costs	16.9	17.0	13.9
Single-family home building direct construction costs	52.0	49.0	65.9
Residential remodeling direct construction costs	0.1	0.0	0.1
Multifamily direct construction costs	2.8	0.6	0.0
Light commercial/industrial direct construction costs	0.2	0.0	0.4
Indirect construction costs	3.1	3.5	1.4
All other costs of goods sold	2.8	2.2	4.4
Total cost of goods sold	77.9	72.3	86.2
Gross profit	**22.1**	**27.7**	**13.8**
Operating expenses			
Financing expense	2.7	1.9	2.0
Sales and marketing expense	4.5	4.7	3.8
General and administrative expense	4.7	4.5	5.8
Owner's compensation	1.1	1.0	2.3
Total operating expenses	13.0	12.0	13.8
Net income before taxes	**9.1**	**15.6**	**0.1**

Table 17 Balance sheet (average in $1,000s)

	All	Top 25%	Bottom 25%
Assets			
Cash	1,286	2,278	1,513
Construction work in progress	14,790	17,753	14,906
Other current assets	1,430	2,563	812
Other assets	1,822	2,365	2,877
Total assets	19,327	24,959	20,109
Liabilities			
Current liabilities	1,773	3,392	1,547
Construction loans	9,417	10,747	12,988
Other liabilities	2,525	1,180	813
Owner's equity	5,613	9,641	4,760
Total liabilities and owner's equity	19,327	24,959	20,109

Builders without land costs
Top and bottom 25% by net income before taxes

Table 18 Income statement (average in $1,000s)

	All	Top 25%	Bottom 25%
Revenue			
Single-family home building	3,636	3,815	3,486
Residential remodeling	322	489	142
Multifamily	796	1,895	0
Light commercial/industrial	24	20	0
All other revenue	89	44	12
Total revenue	4,865	6,263	3,639
Costs of goods sold			
Land costs	0	0	0
Single-family home building direct construction costs	2,958	2,974	2,924
Residential remodeling direct construction costs	196	300	106
Multifamily direct construction costs	671	1,441	0
Light commercial/industrial direct construction costs	14	17	0
Indirect construction costs	233	20	162
All other costs of goods sold	20	70	0
Total cost of goods sold	4,092	4,961	3,192
Gross profit	**773**	**1,302**	**447**
Operating expenses			
Financing expense	24	49	35
Sales and marketing expense	74	79	97
General and administrative expense	325	445	240
Owner's compensation	136	98	150
Total operating expenses	559	670	521
Net income before taxes	214	632	(74)

Table 19 Income statement (% share of revenue)

	All	Top 25%	Bottom 25%
Revenue			
Single-family home building	74.7	60.9	95.8
Residential remodeling	6.6	7.8	3.9
Multifamily	16.4	30.3	0.0
Light commercial/industrial	0.5	0.3	0.0
All other revenue	1.8	0.7	0.3
Total revenue	100.0	100.0	100.0
Costs of goods sold			
Land costs	0.0	0.0	0.0
Single-family home building direct construction costs	60.8	47.5	80.4
Residential remodeling direct construction costs	4.0	4.8	2.9
Multifamily direct construction costs	13.8	23.0	0.0
Light commercial/industrial direct construction costs	0.3	0.3	0.0
Indirect construction costs	4.8	0.3	4.5
All other costs of goods sold	0.4	1.1	0.0
Total cost of goods sold	84.1	79.2	87.7
Gross profit	**15.9**	**20.8**	**12.3**
Operating expenses			
Financing expense	0.5	0.8	1.0
Sales and marketing expense	1.5	1.3	2.7
General and administrative expense	6.7	7.1	6.6
Owner's compensation	2.8	1.6	4.1
Total operating expenses	11.5	10.7	14.3
Net income before taxes	**4.4**	**10.1**	**−2.0**

Table 20 Balance sheet (average in $1,000s)

	All	Top 25%	Bottom 25%
Assets			
Cash	387	709	79
Construction work in progress	1,030	1,757	1,647
Other current assets	241	573	119
Other assets	208	187	89
Total assets	1,865	3,227	1,934
Liabilities			
Current liabilities	680	363	1,081
Construction loans	216	298	475
Other liabilities	354	560	270
Owner's equity	615	2,006	108
Total liabilities and owner's equity	1,865	3,227	1,934

Combination builders
Top and bottom 25% by net income before taxes

Table 21 Income statement (average in $1,000s)

	All	Top 25%	Bottom 25%
Revenue			
Single-family home building	11,871	18,588	9,209
Residential remodeling	140	107	71
Multifamily	711	0	2,732
Light commercial/industrial	306	0	368
All other revenue	703	1,511	479
Total revenue	13,731	20,206	12,859
Costs of goods sold			
Land costs	2,076	2,861	2,300
Single-family home building direct construction costs	7,725	11,502	6,493
Residential remodeling direct construction costs	80	77	50
Multifamily direct construction costs	464	0	1,831
Light commercial/industrial direct construction costs	242	0	307
Indirect construction costs	438	629	425
All other costs of goods sold	247	764	26
Total cost of goods sold	11,272	15,834	11,432
Gross profit	2,459	4,372	1,427
Operating expenses			
Financing expense	327	358	457
Sales and marketing expense	573	836	362
General and administrative expense	694	833	678
Owner's compensation	203	250	117
Total operating expenses	1,798	2,276	1,614
Net income before taxes	661	2,096	(187)

Table 22 Income statement (% share of revenue)

	All	Top 25%	Bottom 25%
Revenue			
Single-family home building	86.5	92.0	71.6
Residential remodeling	1.0	0.5	0.6
Multifamily	5.2	0.0	21.2
Light commercial/industrial	2.2	0.0	2.9
All other revenue	5.1	7.5	3.7
Total revenue	100.0	100.0	100.0
Costs of goods sold			
Land costs	15.1	14.2	17.9
Single-family home building direct construction costs	56.3	56.9	50.5
Residential remodeling direct construction costs	0.6	0.4	0.4
Multifamily direct construction costs	3.4	0.0	14.2
Light commercial/industrial direct construction costs	1.8	0.0	2.4
Indirect construction costs	3.2	3.1	3.3
All other costs of goods sold	1.8	3.8	0.2
Total cost of goods sold	82.1	78.4	88.9
Gross profit	**17.9**	**21.6**	**11.1**
Operating expenses			
Financing expense	2.4	1.8	3.6
Sales and marketing expense	4.2	4.1	2.8
General and administrative expense	5.1	4.1	5.3
Owner's compensation	1.5	1.2	0.9
Total operating expenses	13.1	11.3	12.6
Net income before taxes	**4.8**	**10.4**	**−1.5**

Table 23 Balance sheet (average in $1,000s)

	All	Top 25%	Bottom 25%
Assets			
Cash	354	646	105
Construction work in progress	7,694	11,126	10,949
Other current assets	1,270	881	2,006
Other assets	1,569	1,329	1,410
Total assets	10,888	13,981	14,469
Liabilities			
Current liabilities	2,058	1,805	3,197
Construction loans	5,883	7,211	8,314
Other liabilities	743	1,329	758
Owner's equity	2,203	3,636	2,201
Total liabilities and owner's equity	10,888	13,981	14,469

All single-family builders
Small-volume vs. production builders

Table 24 Income statement (average in $1,000s)

	All	Small-volume	Production
Revenue			
Single-family home building	16,381	3,654	37,464
Residential remodeling	138	190	44
Multifamily	1,393	119	2,458
Light commercial/industrial	127	188	49
All other revenue	647	136	1,605
Total revenue	18,686	4,288	41,620
Costs of goods sold			
Land costs	2,929	365	7,015
Single-family home building direct construction costs	9,809	2,625	21,745
Residential remodeling direct construction costs	90	113	30
Multifamily direct construction costs	866	104	1,535
Light commercial/industrial direct construction costs	98	148	33
Indirect construction costs	605	159	1,302
All other costs of goods sold	402	48	1,099
Total cost of goods sold	14,799	3,562	32,758
Gross profit	**3,887**	**726**	**8,862**
Operating expenses			
Financing expense	462	74	1,085
Sales and marketing expense	827	116	1,879
General and administrative expense	927	249	1,978
Owner's compensation	239	132	417
Total operating expenses	2,456	570	5,358
Net income before taxes	**1,431**	**156**	**3,504**

Table 25 Income statement (% share of revenue)

	All	Small-volume	Production
Revenue			
Single-family home building	87.7	85.2	90.0
Residential remodeling	0.7	4.4	0.1
Multifamily	7.5	2.8	5.9
Light commercial/industrial	0.7	4.4	0.1
All other revenue	3.5	3.2	3.9
Total revenue	100.0	100.0	100.0
Costs of goods sold			
Land costs	15.7	8.5	16.9
Single-family home building direct construction costs	52.5	61.2	52.2
Residential remodeling direct construction costs	0.5	2.6	0.1
Multifamily direct construction costs	4.6	2.4	3.7
Light commercial/industrial direct construction costs	0.5	3.5	0.1
Indirect construction costs	3.2	3.7	3.1
All other costs of goods sold	2.2	1.1	2.6
Total cost of goods sold	79.2	83.1	78.7
Gross profit	**20.8**	**16.9**	**21.3**
Operating expenses			
Financing expense	2.5	1.7	2.6
Sales and marketing expense	4.4	2.7	4.5
General and administrative expense	5.0	5.8	4.8
Owner's compensation	1.3	3.1	1.0
Total operating expenses	13.1	13.3	12.9
Net income before taxes	**7.7**	**3.6**	**8.4**

Table 26 Balance sheet (average in $1,000s)

	All	Small-volume	Production
Assets			
Cash	823	302	1,604
Construction work in progress	9,635	1,853	22,727
Other current assets	1,120	352	2,459
Other assets	1,382	337	3,231
Total assets	12,959	2,845	30,022
Liabilities			
Current liabilities	1,792	776	3,103
Construction loans	6,318	1,232	15,066
Other liabilities	1,438	301	3,482
Owner's equity	3,411	535	8,370
Total liabilities and owner's equity	12,959	2,845	30,022

Builders with land costs
Small-volume vs. production builders

Table 27 Income statement (average in $1,000s)

	All	Small-volume	Production
Revenue			
Single-family home building	25,208	3,914	40,192
Residential remodeling	47	60	37
Multifamily	1,305	26	2,204
Light commercial/industrial	62	53	68
All other revenue	943	114	1,526
Total revenue	27,564	4,168	44,027
Costs of goods sold			
Land costs	4,671	676	7,483
Single-family home building direct construction costs	14,342	2,313	22,806
Residential remodeling direct construction costs	27	31	25
Multifamily direct construction costs	765	21	1,288
Light commercial/industrial direct construction costs	45	44	46
Indirect construction costs	856	124	1,372
All other costs of goods sold	774	64	1,273
Total cost of goods sold	21,481	3,274	34,292
Gross profit	**6,083**	**894**	**9,735**
Operating expenses			
Financing expense	737	141	1,157
Sales and marketing expense	1,241	199	1,973
General and administrative expense	1,299	197	2,074
Owner's compensation	311	143	429
Total operating expenses	3,587	681	5,632
Net income before taxes	**2,496**	**213**	**4,102**

Table 28 Income statement (% share of revenue)

	All	Small-volume	Production
Revenue			
Single-family home building	91.5	93.9	91.3
Residential remodeling	0.2	1.4	0.1
Multifamily	4.7	0.6	5.0
Light commercial/industrial	0.2	1.3	0.2
All other revenue	3.4	2.7	3.5
Total revenue	100.0	100.0	100.0
Costs of goods sold			
Land costs	16.9	16.2	17.0
Single-family home building direct construction costs	52.0	55.5	51.8
Residential remodeling direct construction costs	0.1	0.7	0.1
Multifamily direct construction costs	2.8	0.5	2.9
Light commercial/industrial direct construction costs	0.2	1.1	0.1
Indirect construction costs	3.1	3.0	3.1
All other costs of goods sold	2.8	1.5	2.9
Total cost of goods sold	77.9	78.6	77.9
Gross profit	**22.1**	**21.4**	**22.1**
Operating expenses			
Financing expense	2.7	3.4	2.6
Sales and marketing expense	4.5	4.8	4.5
General and administrative expense	4.7	4.7	4.7
Owner's compensation	1.1	3.4	1.0
Total operating expenses	13.0	16.3	12.8
Net income before taxes	**9.1**	**5.1**	**9.3**

Table 29 Balance sheet (average in $1,000s)

	All	Small-volume	Production
Assets			
Cash	1,286	358	1,956
Construction work in progress	14,790	3,062	23,260
Other current assets	1,430	361	2,201
Other assets	1,822	277	2,937
Total assets	19,327	4,058	30,354
Liabilities			
Current liabilities	1,773	589	2,628
Construction loans	9,417	2,359	14,514
Other liabilities	2,525	363	4,087
Owner's equity	5,613	748	9,126
Total liabilities and owner's equity	19,327	4,058	30,354

Combination builders
Small-volume vs. production builders

Table 30 Income statement (average in $1,000s)

	All	Small-volume	Production
Revenue			
Single-family home building	11,871	3,734	34,021
Residential remodeling	140	167	66
Multifamily	711	26	2,574
Light commercial/industrial	306	419	0
All other revenue	703	190	2,100
Total revenue	13,731	4,536	38,761
Costs of goods sold			
Land costs	2,076	349	6,779
Single-family home building direct construction costs	7,725	2,832	21,046
Residential remodeling direct construction costs	80	92	48
Multifamily direct construction costs	464	0	1,729
Light commercial/industrial direct construction costs	242	330	0
Indirect construction costs	438	153	1,212
All other costs of goods sold	247	61	752
Total cost of goods sold	11,272	3,817	31,567
Gross profit	**2,459**	**719**	**7,194**
Operating expenses			
Financing expense	327	71	1,023
Sales and marketing expense	573	102	1,856
General and administrative expense	694	278	1,827
Owner's compensation	203	129	407
Total operating expenses	1,798	580	5,112
Net income before taxes	**661**	**139**	**2,082**

Table 31 Income statement (% share of revenue)

	All	Small-volume	Production
Revenue			
Single-family home building	86.5	82.3	87.8
Residential remodeling	1.0	3.7	0.2
Multifamily	5.2	0.6	6.6
Light commercial/industrial	2.2	9.2	0.0
All other revenue	5.1	4.2	5.4
Total revenue	100.0	100.0	100.0
Costs of goods sold			
Land costs	15.1	7.7	17.5
Single-family home building direct construction costs	56.3	62.4	54.3
Residential remodeling direct construction costs	0.6	2.0	0.1
Multifamily direct construction costs	3.4	0.0	4.5
Light commercial/industrial direct construction costs	1.8	7.3	0.0
Indirect construction costs	3.2	3.4	3.1
All other costs of goods sold	1.8	1.3	1.9
Total cost of goods sold	82.1	84.1	81.4
Gross profit	**17.9**	**15.9**	**18.6**
Operating expenses			
Financing expense	2.4	1.6	2.6
Sales and marketing expense	4.2	2.2	4.8
General and administrative expense	5.1	6.1	4.7
Owner's compensation	1.5	2.8	1.1
Total operating expenses	13.1	12.8	13.2
Net income before taxes	4.8	3.1	5.4

Table 32 Balance sheet (average in $1,000s)

	All	Small-volume	Production
Assets			
Cash	354	219	730
Construction work in progress	7,694	1,759	24,180
Other current assets	1,270	505	3,396
Other assets	1,569	483	4,584
Total assets	10,888	2,967	32,889
Liabilities			
Current liabilities	2,058	1,015	4,955
Construction loans	5,883	1,124	19,103
Other liabilities	743	295	1,987
Owner's equity	2,203	533	6,844
Total liabilities and owner's equity	10,888	2,967	32,889

Appendix

II

Survey
Instrument

Grant Thornton

Please report on your **fiscal year 2006 operations**.

Please Fax Your Reply to **1-800-822-2102 (Toll Free)** or 202-266-8575.

Or, mail to: NAHB Economics Dept. Attn: Rose Quint,1201 15th Street, N.W., Washington, DC
20005

IMPORTANT: Complete and return your survey by **MAY 1, 2007**, and you get a **FREE Copy** of the published *Cost of Doing Business Study*.

I. FIRM'S PROFILE

1. In the first column, <u>please indicate your firm's main operation during</u> fiscal year 2006 and write in the percentage of your business that operation represents. In the second column, <u>please indicate all other operations</u> your firm participated in during fiscal year 2006 and write in the percentage of your business those operations represent.

	Main operation (Check ONE only)	All other operations (Check ALL applicable)	Percent of Your Business
Single-family production builder	❏	❏	_____ %
Single-family custom builder (on owner's lot)	❏	❏	_____ %
Single-family custom builder (on builder's lot)	❏	❏	_____ %
Multifamily builder (condo/co-op units)	❏	❏	_____ %
Multifamily builder (for-rent units)	❏	❏	_____ %
Land developer	❏	❏	_____ %
Residential remodeling/rehabilitation	❏	❏	_____ %
Other (specify)	❏	❏	_____ %
		Total:	**100%**

2. Is the operating head of your firm an owner or a salaried executive?

❏ Principal owner   ❏ Salaried executive only (not a principal owner)
❏ Sole owner   ❏ Other (specify) _____

3. How many years has your firm been in the residential construction business?
_____year(s)

The Business Management & Information Technology Committee would like to thank our *Cost of Doing Business Study* Sponsor:

II. FINANCIAL INFORMATION

4. Income Statement

*Each code number refers to the NAHB Chart of Accounts, found at www.nahb.org/chart		
Revenue from Operations		
Single-Family Home Building Revenue [3100-3125]	$	
Residential Remodeling Revenue [3130]	$	
Multifamily Revenue [3140]	$	
Light Commercial/Industrial Revenue [3150]	$	
All Other Revenue [3000, 3050, 3160-3490]	$	
Total Company Revenue [sum of the previous five entries]		$
Expenses		
Land Costs [3550]	$	
Single-Family Home Building Direct Construction Costs [3600, 3610, 3620, 3625] (permits, labor with burden, trade contractors, material costs, other unit-specific construction costs)	$	
Residential Remodeling Direct Construction Costs [3800-3899]	$	
Multifamily Direct Construction Costs [3640]	$	
Light Commercial/Industrial Direct Construction Costs [3650]	$	
Indirect Construction Costs [4000-4990] (job site and non-unit specific construction costs; include job supervision, estimating, purchasing and design personnel, warranty costs, construction vehicles, tools, and any other indirect costs)	$	
All Other Costs of Goods Sold (cost of sales related to items that fall under "All Other Revenue")	$	
Financing Expense [5000-5990] (points and interest on all business loans)	$	
Sales and Marketing Expense [6000-6990] (commissions, sales salaries and burden, advertising and sales promotion, and model home maintenance)	$	
General and Administrative Expense [8000-8990] (salaries, payroll taxes, and benefits of non job-related personnel; office & computer expense, vehicles, travel, entertainment, taxes, insurance, professional services, and depreciation) (exclude owner's compensation)	$	
Owner's Compensation [8010] (owner's salary, draws, bonuses, and benefits)	$	
Net Income Before Taxes [total company revenue minus total expenses]		$

5. Balance Sheet

[Each code number refers to the NAHB Chart of Accounts, found at www.nahb.org/chart]			
Assets		**Liabilities and Owner's Equity**	
Cash [1000-1090]	$	Current Liabilities [2000-2490]	$
Construction Work in Progress [1400-1490]	$	Construction Loans [2230]	$
Other Current Assets [1500-1690]	$	Other Liabilities [2510, 2530-2890]	$
Other Assets [1700-1990]	$	Owner's Equity [2900-2990]	$
Total Assets	$	Total Liabilities and Owner's Equity	$

III. CONSTRUCTION PROFILE

6. Of the total number of single family-units closed in fiscal year 2006, how many were pre-sold, speculative, and/or built on others' land (customer lots)? (*If none in a category, please write zero.*)

	Single-Family Units Closed
Presold (on builder's lot)	_____
Speculative	_____
Built on others' land (customers' lots)	_____
TOTAL	_____

7. How many single-family units closed in fiscal year 2006 were built on lots your firm developed? How many were built on developed lots your firm purchased? How many were built on others' land (customers' lots)? (*If none in a category, please write zero.*)

	Single-Family Units Closed
Built on land my firm developed	_____
Built on developed lots my firm purchased	_____
Built on others' land (customers' lots)	_____
TOTAL	_____

8. Of the single-family units closed in fiscal year 2006, how many were stick-built, modular, panelized, and/or pre-cut units? *(If none in a category, please write zero)*

	Single-Family Units
Stick-built	_____
Modular	_____
Panelized	_____
Pre-cut	_____
Other (specify)	_____
TOTAL	_____

9. Comments/Explanation:

_____

_____

_____

_____

Optional: Please provide contact information so we can send you your free copy of the study. **This and all other information you provide will be kept strictly confidential.**

Name: _____

Company: _____

Street Address: _____

City: _____ State: _____ Zip: _____

Phone: _____

E-mail: _____

FAX Back (Toll-Free) to: 800-822-2102 – or, 202-266-8575

OR – simply mail back in the **postage-paid envelope** we've enclosed for your convenience.

Questions? Please contact **Rose Quint at 800-368-5242 x8527**

Appendix

Tax Tips
from
Grant Thornton

Business owners and managers face complex tax issues that can strain resources and drain profits. Grant Thornton's tax professionals offer

10 Tax Tips for Construction Contractors...

... that can help you manage your tax burden.

1. **Review the Small Business and Work Opportunity Tax Act.** The Act expanded the "kiddie" tax provisions even further, for 2008 individual returns. These rules now apply to most children over 18 years of age who are full time students.
2. **Review your deferred compensation plans.** Complex new rules are in effect this year, even though the deadline for revising plan documents has been extended to the end of 2008. These rules affect plans that result in a compensation deferral and, if violated, can accelerate taxation to recipients, plus the payment of interest and penalties.
3. **Review your transfer pricing agreements.** Many states and foreign jurisdictions are reviewing inter-company transactions whether it be for royalties or management charges. In addition to having the proper inter-company charges in place you also need the proper back up documentation.
4. **Determine if your company can lower property taxes.** A property tax review would ensure that all real and intangible property is excluded from the personal property tax base. In addition, there may be opportunities to lower the property tax valuations on your real property. The review would not only generate savings in the first year, but future years as well.
5. **Examine your capital asset depreciation methods and lives.** "Catch-up" deductions are possible on under-depreciated existing assets. You may be able to write off 100 percent of the under-depreciated amount in the current tax year without amending past returns by filing an automatic change in accounting method.
6. **Obtain a marketing edge by offering your customers more.** Work with Grant Thornton to provide a turn-key cost segregation study to your customer with your completed project. We can assist in analyzing and appropriately classifying capital assets associated with the project into the most tax-beneficial depreciable lives.
7. **Analyze the structure of your business.** How your business is organized can have a major impact on the amount of taxes you pay, especially in the areas of state, local and unemployment taxation. Consider the benefits of restructuring your business (for example, by establishing a partnership to provide inter-company services), while at the same time potentially reducing state, local and unemployment tax liabilities.
8. **Consider establishing a separate entity to own and lease fixed assets used in your business.** Often referred to as "leasing companies" or "procurement companies," these entities help manage your assets and may significantly reduce your sales and use tax – a tax you collect and remit regardless of whether your company is profitable.
9. **Review your state filing requirements.** Multiple states have switched to a unitary filing requirement. For example, New York and Texas are switching in 2007 with Michigan to follow in 2008. In addition, in 2007, Texas is switching to a margin tax and in 2008, Michigan is replacing its single business tax with an income and margin tax. State tax law changes may have a significant impact on your state tax liability.
10. **Review your accounting methods.** The operations of contractors can result in the need for multiple methods of accounting. Be sure that you are using appropriate and advantageous methods. Also, ask Grant Thornton how we may assist you to defer revenue on projects where you use subcontractors.

Business owners and managers face complex tax issues that can strain resources and drain profits. Grant Thornton's tax professionals offer

10 Tax Tips for Real Estate Developers and Investors...

... that can help you manage your tax burden.

1. **Understand your partnership or LLC agreement.** Do you truly understand your partnership or LLC operating agreement? Do you know if the allocations among members have "substantial economic effect"? Do you know what a qualified income offset provision is? Do you understand minimum gain? In real estate matters, operating agreements typically address these and other important tax issues. Chances are your agreement is written with such issues in mind, and it is important that you understand them completely.

2. **Properly account for your lease income.** You may be accounting for your lease income for tax purposes based on the cash received or on the terms of the lease agreement. However, a Code section specifically addressing leases may require the income to be accounted for differently.

3. **Maintain three sets of partnership books.** If your entity is a partnership, are you maintaining three sets of books? If not, you may not be following the required tax rules and your allocations among partners may not be valid.

4. **Determine if you are a dealer or an investor.** Do you know your status as either a dealer or an investor for tax purposes? Proper planning upfront will ensure the desired treatment upon disposition of the property.

5. **Allocate land cost to your benefit.** To defer income upon the sale of parcels from a tract of land purchased, proper allocation of the cost among the various parcels must be done. The IRS requires that the cost be "equitably apportioned." But how? There are several methods available that should be considered when allocating cost.

6. **Color your building green.** You should take advantage where possible of a special deduction and credit for so-called green buildings.

7. **Sometimes don't even think about it.** The tax law requires that many soft costs, including property taxes, be capitalized if it is "reasonable likely" that a structure will be built or the land developed. So be careful in documenting your intent as it may result in capitalization of some expenses.

8. **Take full advantage of depreciation.** Has your company recently undertaken new construction projects, expansions or renovations? Substantial long-term savings could result from a cost segregation study which categorizes your assets into the appropriate and most tax-advantaged depreciable lives.

9. **Beware of what you do with an installment note.** When an installment note received in connection with a sale is disposed of, the deferred gain will be triggered. In addition, the pledging of the installment note or the transfer of the note to an LLC might be deemed a disposition.

10. **Reward key executives.** Do you have key executives that you would like to give a piece of "the action" as a member of your real estate partnership? If structured properly, this may be accomplished without immediate income recognition by these executives.

Hospitality property owners and managers face complex tax issues that can strain resources and impact profits. Grant Thornton's tax professionals offer

10 Tax Tips for the Hospitality Industry...

... that can help you manage your tax burden.

1. **Review the Small Business and Work Opportunity Tax Act.** The Act offers two changes to the tip credit which is the employer portion of Social Security tax paid for cash tips. Effective for 2007, the credit is not affected by the minimum wage increase and can offset the alternative minimum tax.
2. **Assess Tax Credit Potential.** Your Grant Thornton tax professional can inform you of specific tax credits that may be relevant to your business. For example, the tip credit and certain general business credits, such as the welfare-to-work credit and the work opportunity tax credit, can provide significant tax savings for the hospitality industry.
3. **Review your deferred compensation plans.** Complex new rules are in effect and should be in place by the end of 2007. These rules affect plans that result in a compensation deferral and, if violated, can accelerate taxation to recipients, plus the payment of interest and penalties.
4. **Review your state filing requirements.** Multiple states have switched to a unitary filing requirement. For example, New York and Texas are switching in 2007 with Michigan to follow in 2008. In addition, in 2007, Texas is switching to a margin tax and in 2008, Michigan is replacing its single business tax with an income and margin tax. State tax law changes may have a significant impact on your state tax liability.
5. **Analyze the structure of your business.** How your business is organized can have a major impact on the amount of taxes you pay. Consider the benefits of restructuring your business to address inequities in unemployment taxation or state taxation. Also, establishing a partnership to provide inter-company services may create potentially favorable income tax results.
6. **Consider establishing a separate entity to own and lease fixed assets used in your business.** Often referred to as "leasing companies" or "procurement companies," these entities can help manage your assets and may significantly reduce your sales and use tax – a tax you collect and remit regardless of whether your company is profitable.
7. **Determine if your company can lower property taxes.** A property tax review would ensure that all real and intangible property is excluded from the personal property tax base. In addition, there may be opportunities to lower the property tax valuations on your real property. The review would not only generate savings in the first year, but future years as well.
8. **Review your accounting methods.** The operation of restaurants, hotels, and other hospitality-based companies can result in the need for multiple methods of accounting. Be sure that you are using the most appropriate and advantageous methods. For example, there is an exception for inventoriable goods, which includes gift certificates, that allows for a two year deferral under regulation section 1.451-5 for advanced payments.
9. **Review your transfer pricing agreements.** Many states are reviewing intercompany transactions whether it be for royalties or management charges. In addition to having the proper inter-company charges in place you also need the proper back up documentation.
10. **Select the Most Beneficial Depreciable Lives for Your Assets.** Grant Thornton can perform a cost classification study on your current fixed asset records or construction activities in order to appropriately identify the most tax-beneficial recovery period for those assets.

biztools
Business Management & Information Technology Committee

About the NAHB Business Management & Information Technology Committee

The NAHB Business Management & Information Technology Committee is dedicated to improving the business management skills of NAHB's builder members to enhance their competitiveness, profitability, and professionalism.

In accordance with the objectives of the NAHB strategic plan, the committee makes policy recommendations on business management issues, develops educational programs, writes and publishes manuals, conducts business management research, and provides consultation to other committees.

The Committee's mission statement is:

> *"To serve as the leading resource to the building industry in the areas of management, finance, information technology, operations, and human resources."*

The members of the 2007 Business Management & Information Technology Committee are as follows:

Antonio Giordano, Chair, Mast Construction
Randy Noel, Vice Chair, Reve Inc.
John Barrows, CGB, GMB, 2nd Vice Chair, J. Barrows Inc.
David Asbridge, Highmark Builders
Rex Bouldin, Pinecrest Builders
Catherine Foushee, Construction IT Group
Maggie Geoffroy, Construction Data Control Inc.
Alan Hanbury, Jr., CGR, CAPS, House of Hanbury Builders Inc.
Steve Hays, Rubin Brown LLP
John Jones, SoftPlan Systems Inc.
Joel B. Katz, GMB, CPA, Katz Builders Inc.
Jeremy Larsen, NCHI Liaison, Sage Software
Steve Lewkowitz, Pivotal Corp.
Peter Merrill, Construction Dispute Resolution Services LLC.
Richard Miles, Dogwood Homes
Thomas Mullen, CMP, MIRM, Thomas E. Mullen & Associates
Ronald Rohrbach, EOC liaison, HBA of Berks County
Larry Rolwes, Rolwes Homes Inc.
Manny Schatz, CAASH, CMP, MIRM, Professional Builder Services Inc.
Tim Shigley, CGR, GMB, Shigley Construction Co.
Thomas Vetter, CMP, CSP, MCSP, MIRM, Move
Gary Wilkerson, Riverview Homes Inc.
Clarion Wysocki, Rusty Wysocki Building Co. Inc.

ABOUT THE NATIONAL ASSOCIATION OF HOME BUILDERS

The National Association of Home Builders is a Washington-based trade association representing more than 235,000 members involved in home building, remodeling, multifamily construction, property management, trade contracting, design, housing finance, building product manufacturing, and other aspects of residential and light commercial construction. Known as "the voice of the housing industry," NAHB is affiliated with more than 800 state and local home builders associations around the country. NAHB's builder members construct about 80 percent of all new residential units, supporting one of the largest engines of economic growth in the country: housing.

 Join the National Association of Home Builders by joining your local home builders association. Visit www.nahb.org/join or call 800-368-5242, x0, for information on state and local associations near you. Great member benefits include:

- Access to the **National Housing Resource Center** and its collection of electronic databases, books, journals, videos, and CDs. Call 800-368-5254, x8296 or e-mail nhrc@nahb.org
- **Nation's Building News**, the weekly e-newsletter containing industry news. Visit www.nahb.org/nbn
- **Extended access to www.nahb.org** when members log in. Visit www.nahb.org/login
- **Business Management Tools** for members only that are designed to help you improve strategic planning, time management, information technology, customer service, and increase profits through effective business management. Visit www.nahb.org/biztools
- **Council membership**:
  - **Building Systems Council**: www.nahb.org/buildingsystems
  - **Commercial Builders Council**: www.nahb.org/commercial
  - **Building Systems Council's Concrete Home Building Council**: www.nahb.org/concrete
  - **Multifamily Council**: www.nahb.org/multifamily
  - **National Sales & Marketing Council**: www.nahb.org/nsmc
  - **NAHB Remodelers**: www.nahb.org/remodelers
  - **Women's Council**: www.nahb.org/womens
  - **50+ Housing Council**: www.nahb.org/50plus

 BuilderBooks, the book publishing arm of NAHB, publishes inspirational and educational products for the housing industry and offers a variety of books, software, brochures, and more in English and Spanish. Visit www.BuilderBooks.com or call 800-223-2665. NAHB members save at least 10% on every book.

 BuilderBooks Digital Delivery offers over 30 publications, forms, contracts, and checklists that are instantly delivered in electronic format to your desktop. Visit www.BuilderBooks.com and click on Digital Delivery.

 The **Member Advantage Program** offers NAHB members discounts on products and services such as computers, automobiles, payroll services, and much more. Keep more of your hard-earned revenue by cashing in on the savings today. Visit www.nahb.org/ma for a comprehensive overview of all available programs.